THE MAGIC OF ESOT:
*The Fabulous New Instrument
Of Corporate Finance*

THE MAGIC OF ESOT:
The Fabulous New Instrument of Corporate Finance

by

ROBERT A. FRISCH, CLU

FARNSWORTH PUBLISHING COMPANY, INC.
Rockville Centre, N.Y. 11570

© 1975 Robert A. Frisch, CLU
All rights reserved.
First printing.
Library of Congress Catalog Card No. 75-13780.
ISBN 0-87863-108-9.
Manufactured in the United States of America.
No part of this book may be reproduced
without the written permission of the publisher.

For Leona, Dana, and Randi

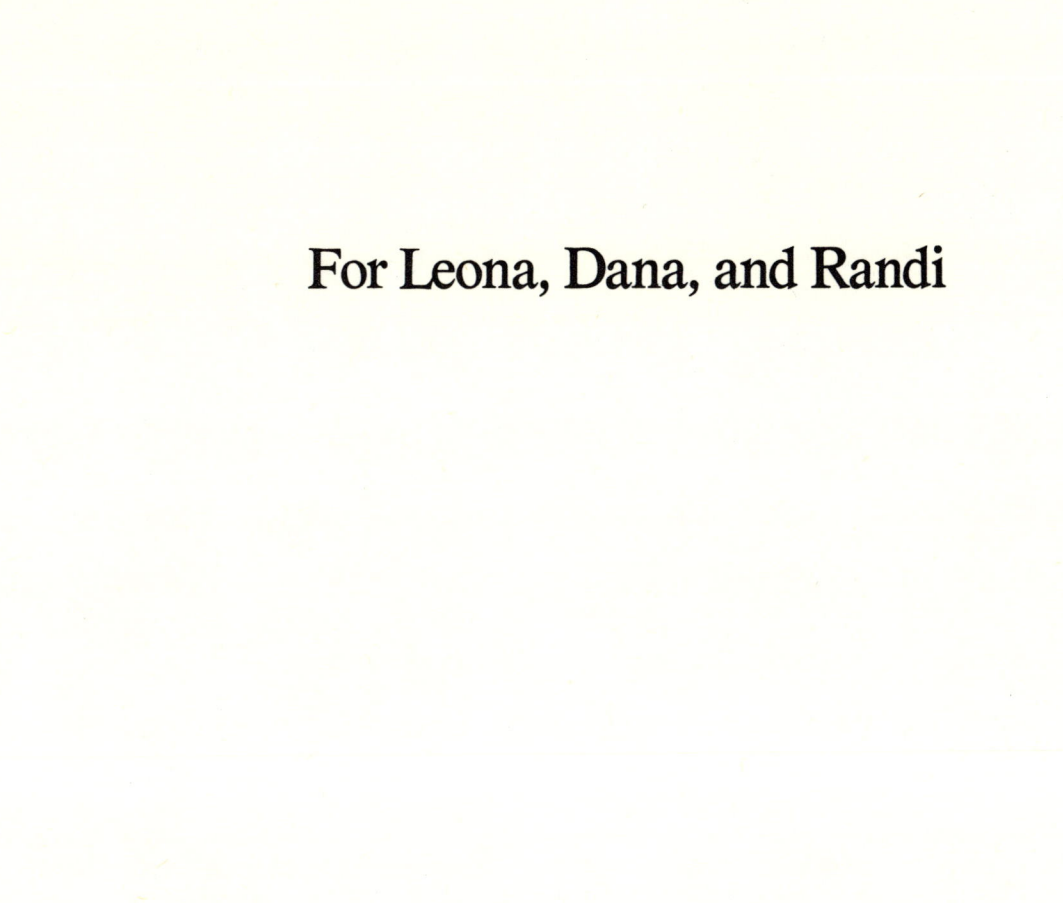

For Leana, Dana, and Randi

ACKNOWLEDGEMENT

Herbert S. Botsford, CPA, Partner
Joel S. Marcus, J.D., CPA, Associate
of Arthur Young & Company

for valuable contributions relative to tax aspects of Employee Stock Ownership Trusts.

Prologue

It is with a great deal of enthusiasm that I tell you about the creative aspects of the Employee Stock Ownership Trust.

> To my knowledge there is no other conceptual device that lends itself so magnificently to corporate and stockholder financial planning as well as capital financing, while providing an exceptional employee benefit program that is without peer.

As of this date, relatively few corporations have taken advantage of the ESOT. The reason, I suspect, is that no one has brought to the attention of most decision-makers the creative implications an ESOT might have for their companies.

> Although some Employee Stock Ownership Plans have been in effect for more than twenty years, they are referred to by this name in the Internal Revenue Code for the first time in the Employee Retirement Income Security Act of 1974.

Tax regulations change from time to time and their interpretations vary from IRS District Director to District Director.

> This book is sold with the understanding that neither the author nor the publisher is rendering, or intends to render, any professional advice. A corporation should implement an ESOT or engage in any technique discussed in this book only after thorough consultation with its legal counsel, accountant, and life insurance advisor.

After reviewing the ideas presented in the pages that follow, I am confident that many companies and their advisors will investigate the wide range of uses for ESOT which may solve monumental problems effectively and economically.

ROBERT A. FRISCH

TABLE OF CONTENTS

Prologue	i
1. What Is An ESOT?	7
2. Control Of Stock In The Trust	13
3. Which Way To Go—Public Or Private?	19
4. How To Increase Working Capital And Cash Flow Through An ESOT While Remaining Private	25
5. How Stockholders Can "Cash-Out" While Still Retaining Control	31
6. How The Corporation Can Repay Loan Principal And Interest With Pre-Tax Dollars	35
7. How Corporations Can Make Acquisitions With Pre-Tax Dollars	39
8. How To Have An ESOT, Profit-Sharing Plan, And A Pension Plan With No Net Cash Outlay	41
9. How It May Be Possible To Use Profit-Sharing Assets To Increase Corporate Working Capital	45
10. How It May Be Possible To Obtain A Refund Of Taxes Paid In Prior Years	49
11. How To Transfer Stock After Death	51
12. The Frisch Plan—A Way To Fund An ESOT/Stockholder Buy-Sell Agreement Or Acquire ESOT Keyman Insurance With No Net After-Tax Cash Outlay	53
13. The Stock Retirement Agreement Vs. The ESOT Buy-Out	61
14. The 303 Redemption Is Good—But ESOT May Be Far Better. Here's Why:	63
15. How Large Stockholders In Public Corporations Can Sell Their Stock Without A Secondary Offering	67
16. How Minority Stockholders Can Be Enticed To Sell Their Stock	69
17. How To Remove Assets From The Estate—Private Annuity Or ESOT?	73
18. How ESOT's Can Help Franchisors And Franchisees	77
19. How To Get Personal And Corporate Tax Deductions That Exceed The Value Of Your Gift	81
20. How A Corporation Can Facilitate A Divestiture With An ESOT	85
21. How A Corporation Can Help Avoid A Takeover	89
22. How A Public Company Can Go Private	93
23. How Banks Can Increase Their Lending Capacity Through An ESOT	97

24. How To Increase The Capital Base Of A Savings And Loan Association With An ESOT	101
25. Why Stockbrokers Tell Their Prospects Or Clients About The ESOT	103
26. How Investment Bankers And Venture Capital Specialists Can Increase Their Effectiveness Through ESOT's	105
27. How Life Or Casualty Insurance Agencies And Companies Can Grow With ESOT's	107
28. Practical Ways To Use Life Insurance In ESOT's— All With Pre-Tax Corporate Dollars	109
29. Disadvantages Of An ESOT	115
30. The Social Significance Of ESOT	117
31. History Of ESOT	119
32. Implementing The ESOT	121
33. Profile Of Likely Candidates For ESOT	123
34. Employee Stock Ownership Trust Feasibility Checklist	125
35. Corp, Inc., Feasibility Study	127
36. How Some Corporations May Be Able To Get Preferential Consideration For A Low Interest Government-Backed Loan Through ESOT's	139
37. Questions And Answers	141
38. Sample Of An Employee Stock Ownership Plan	145
39. Sample Of An Employee Stock Ownership Trust Agreement	167
40. Summary	181
Appendix	183

1.

What Is An ESOT?

Corporations can increase their working capital, cash flow, and achieve other beneficial financial results through the vehicle of an Employee Stock Ownership Trust (ESOT). In discussing ESOT, we are really reviewing a means of "going private"—or—"going public internally."

ESOT's are deferred compensation Trusts created by corporations for the exclusive benefit of employees. They qualify for favored tax treatment under the same general area of the Internal Revenue Code that relates to corporate pension, profit-sharing, and stock bonus plans and trusts.

What An ESOT Can Do For A Corporation And Its Stockholders

Here is a partial list of benefits that can accrue to a company and its owners through the implementation of an Employee Stock Ownership Trust:

1. Recover income tax paid in prior years;
2. Liquidate existing debt or arrange new financing so that not only interest, but principal as well, is repaid with pre-tax dollars;
3. Provide a market for stock—even stock of a closely-held corporation—so that stockholders can sell their stock to the ESOT at prices somewhat comparable to similar public companies;
4. Allow the corporation to sell its stock to the ESOT thus generally increasing cash flow, working capital and net worth with pre-tax dollars;
5. Convert an existing profit-sharing plan to an ESOT, where permitted, so that the funds can be used to buy shares in the corporation;
6. Make acquisitions or divestitures with pre-tax dollars;
7. Public companies can improve their control of outstanding shares through the ESOT;
8. Key stockholders can solve many estate planning problems with pre-tax dollars through the ESOT;
9. Improve employee morale.

Here Is How The ESOT Works

The Internal Revenue Code permits a corporation to create a Trust to which the company makes tax-deductible contributions for the benefit of certain employees who meet eligibility criteria, the contributions being limited basically to 15% of the payroll of those employees. Under certain guidelines for an ESOT the limit may possibly be increased to 25%.

> The Employee Stock Ownership Trust is designed to invest in company stock or employer real property and to make ultimate distributions in stock to the participants. It can, therefore, be 100% invested in employer stock, whereas such stock ownership by most pension and profit-sharing Trusts is limited to 10% of Trust assets.

An ESOT is permitted to leverage its investments whereas the Internal Revenue Code does not condone a pension or profit-sharing Trust's borrowing money to acquire stock or other assets. It is this feature which makes ESOT's so useful in debt financing. The fact that corporate contributions can be made to ESOT's regardless of profits is ideal for debt servicing. Contributions to profit-sharing plans must come from profits.

Example:

> Corp, Inc., whose payroll for the participating employees totals one million dollars, contributes $150,000 of authorized but unissued stock to the ESOT, thereby deducting $150,000 from taxes. Assuming the corporation's Federal and State income tax bracket is 54% (this figure varies by state), the company saves $81,000 in taxes, thereby increasing its cash flow and working capital by this amount that would otherwise have gone to pay taxes. The accounts of employees who are participants in the ESOT are credited with shares of the Trust assets.

If the $150,000 were contributed to a profit-sharing plan instead of to an ESOT, the contribution would be in cash. A corporation in the 54% combined Federal and State income tax bracket would save $81,000 in taxes but would pay out a net after-tax amount of $69,000, reducing working capital by that amount.

Summary of major differences between ESOT's and profit-sharing Trusts

1. ESOT's can be fully invested in qualified employer securities. PST stock investments are limited to those with a dividend history, and are subject to a diversification requirement. Maximum of 10% of PST assets can be in employer stock.

2. Distribution to ESOT participants must be in employer stock. Distribution from PST is generally in cash.

3. Corporation can make contribution to an ESOT irrespective of profits.

    Corporation must make contributions to a PST only out of current or accumulated profits.

MODEL:

ESOT Compared With A Profit-Sharing Trust

Assumption: Corporation in 54% combined Federal and State Tax bracket; pre-tax earnings $250,000; covered payroll $1 million. 15% contribution to Trust.

CORPORATION → $150,000 STOCK → ESOT

Corporation's cash flow is increased by the amount of taxes saved, $81,000 (54% of $150,000).

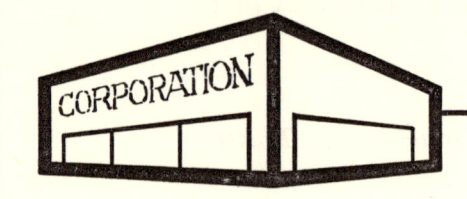

CORPORATION → $150,000 CASH → PROFIT SHARING TRUST

Corporation's cash flow is decreased by the contribution less the tax savings ($150,000 - $81,000 = $69,000).

Summary:

Contribution of newly-issued stock instead of cash to a qualified Trust keeps the cash at work in the corporation.

MODEL:

Effect Of Contribution To Qualified Trusts On Company Statement

	ESOT	Profit-Sharing Trust	No Qualified Trust
Pre-Tax Income	$250,000	$250,000	$250,000
Less Contribution:	150,000 (STOCK)	150,000 (CASH)	0
Net Taxable Inc.	100,000	100,000	250,000
Income Tax (Federal & State)	54,000	54,000	135,000
Net After-Tax Inc.	46,000	46,000	115,000
Cash Flow	$196,000*	$ 46,000	$115,000

*The $150,000 contribution remains at work in the corporation.

2.

Control Of Stock In The Trust

The Employee Stock Ownership Plan (ESOP) is designed for the exclusive benefit of employees and provides deferred compensation for participants. The shares of stock in the Trust are voted by the Trustee at the direction of the administrative committee which is, in turn, appointed by the Corporation's Board of Directors. The Trustees, the administrative committee, and, in some instances, the board, are fiduciaries in which capacity they must adhere to prudent practices.

Who Are The Participants In An Esot?

Eligibility for participation in the ESOT must be in accordance with acceptable IRS criteria. Typical eligibility requirements might be:

All Full Time Employees,
1 Year of Service.

How Are Shares In The ESOT Allocated?

A fairly common allocation formula is based upon length of service and/or basic compensation such as:

... one point for each year of service and,
... one point for each $100 of annual compensation.

Another formula might be simply a matter of allocating shares of the Trust in the same proportion that the employee's salary bears to the total covered payroll.

The Plan could be integrated with Social Security. For example, the contribution formula could be 7% of the eligible employers' compensation in excess of the salary level on which Social Security is based. This would tend to concentrate the benefits of the ESOT on the more highly compensated employees.

MODEL:

Allocation Of Shares To Corp, Inc., Employee Stock Ownership Trust Participants

Payroll of ESOT Participants: $1,000,000
Corporation Contribution To ESOT: 15% of payroll, or $150,000.

Employee	Salary	% of Payroll	Amount Credited To Account
Vice President	$40,000	4.0%	$6,000 (4% x $150,000)
Department Head	15,000	1.5%	$2,250 (1.5% x $150,000)
Clerk	8,000	0.8%	$1,200 (0.8% x $150,000)
Others (in aggregate)	937,000		
Total:	$1,000,000		

Vesting of Employees

> Vesting refers to the shares of the Trust to which an employee would be entitled in the event of termination, death, or retirement. If, for example, an ESOT vests 10% per year, an employee who terminates after four years would be 40% vested and would be entitled to 40% of the shares apportioned to his account in the Trust.

This could be given to him at the time of termination or, if the Trust permits, the committee could direct the Trustee to make a distribution at normal retirement age. The Trustee would hold onto the assets of the terminating employee's account until he reaches normal retirement age, at which time he would receive his shares of the Trust. The non-vested portion of his account, the forfeiture, reverts to the remaining participants.

What Happens Upon Death?

> The vesting treatment as it pertains to death or total disability of a participant varies from total vesting of his account to a distribution of the amount that is vested up to that time.

It is commonplace to consider a participant fully vested in the event of death, in which case the total amount in his account would be payable by the Trustee to his beneficiary.

What Happens At Retirement?

> The stock held by the ESOT becomes the basis of retirement security for the participating employees. They ultimately receive their distributions in the form of stock. There are various options that might be built into the ESOT. Some District Directors of Internal Revenue have disallowed provisions that other District Directors have approved and vice versa. For example: The employee might be given a put to sell the stock to the Trust or to the corporation at its then evaluated price. The ESOT could obtain the necessary cash from the bank if it requires additional liquidity. This

technique will be discussed. Participants cannot be required to sell back to the Trust, or to the corporation, stock they receive from the Trust at the time of termination.

The Trust is sometimes given first right of refusal to buy the stock from the employee, the corporation second right, and the stockholders third right of refusal. These options are applicable only if the same treatment is accorded all stock of that class whether or not it was ever held by the Trust.

How Employee Is Taxed

The employee is not subject to tax on the employer's contribution to his account or on the earnings of the Trust during his working years with the employer. He is not subject to taxation on the unrealized appreciation of the securities in his account at the time of distribution. It is only when he sells the securities that the appreciation above the ESOT's cost basis is taxed as a capital gain.

> If securities are distributed in a lump sum to a terminated participant, he is taxed on the Trust's cost basis for the stock. The tax is at ordinary income rates with ten-year averaging where the distribution is attributable to post-1973 service. Long-term capital gains prevail on distributions which represent pre-1974 service.

Distribution to a terminated employee can be made in increments rather than in a lump sum. The amounts so distributed are taxable to the ex-participants as ordinary income, but spreading the withdrawal over a period of years will tend to soften the tax bite. It is assumed here that the employees do not contribute to the plan.

> Upon death, the participant's account, if payable to a named beneficiary, is not includable in his estate for federal estate tax purposes.

3.

Which Way To Go—Public Or Private?

The company decision-maker should consider the pros and cons of being a public or a private company. His conclusion can have a lasting effect on all of the corporation's subsequent activities.

Difficulties In Getting Cash Out Of A Public Company

One of the primary reasons for "going public" is the anticipation that the stock will sell at a substantial multiple of earnings, thereby enabling the founders to sell some or all of their shares at a tremendous capital gain.

> If a major stockholder-officer of a company that has been public for some time wishes to sell a block of his shares on the open market he must do so through a "secondary offering" preceded by a prospectus. The very fact that Mr. Big is selling often has an adverse effect on the price of the stock when a secondary is announced. He

may not realize as much cash as he would like. The underwriters of the "secondary offering" also get a significant share of his pie.

Logic Of The Public Marketplace

Cash-out at a proper price can be tricky in a public company. In recent years, stock of sound public companies with good earnings track records have sometimes sold below liquidation or book value.

> The pricing of publicly owned stock is in the laps of the gods—the public. There is little scientific basis for the price of a share of common stock on any given day. A famine in the Far East or a show of strength of a major or a minor power—factors which have no bearing on the manufacture of widgits—can have as much effect on the price as an increase in the cost of the company's raw materials. There is little rhyme or reason to pricing public stock.

Certainly, in this world of immeasurable complications, it is impossible for anyone—much less all the average stockholders—to weigh in any scientific fashion the impact these many factors will have on the market price of a given stock.

Difficulties In Getting Capital Out Of The Private Company

One of the joys in owning a corporation comes from the feeling of security occasioned by capital ownership. The majority stockholder of a closely-held (non-public) corporation is often little more than just another highly-paid employee who has created a taxable liability in his estate equal to the value of his stock in the company. There is no practical way that he can get the capital out of the company for personal enjoyment while he is still alive unless he is willing to sell the company.

> He cannot count on selling shares during his lifetime without giving up control. Few investors would be willing to purchase a minority interest in a closely-held corporation. They would realize that there is no reasonable assurance of obtaining a return on their investment or even recapturing principal.

The only way a minority stockholder could get an income from his stock investment is via a dividend.

> There is little likelihood of the company's paying a dividend. Why should it? The corporation cannot deduct the dividend and the stockholder pays taxes on the dividend when he receives it—*double taxation*. No dividend—no investment return to the minority stockholder unless he sells the shares.

To whom would the minority stockholder sell the stock? To another stockholder? Probably not. He might find the majority stockholder to be the only potential buyer. He would be quite at the mercy of the majority stockholder who may not feel the need to buy the stock since he has control without further cash expenditure. If the major stockholder does buy the stock, he may do so at a depreciated price.

> For all practical purposes then, the majority stockholder would have little hope of getting cash out of the business by selling a few shares to investors. He would, in all probability, have to relinquish control in order to transform his stock into cash.

Getting Working Capital For The Private Company

> If it *were* possible to find the potential buyers, the SEC rules preclude selling corporate stock to more than a limited number of individuals without the costly preparation of a prospectus, onerous filings and disclosure mechanisms.

If the founder wished to raise $250,000 of working capital and did not want to become involved with SEC requirements, he would be obliged to limit the offering to twenty-five investors. Each participant in the offering would have to purchase, on average, ten thousand dollars worth of stock to achieve the goal.

> Instead of buying stock in a private company with no near-term marketability, the investor could have diversified his ten thousand

dollar investment by purchasing stock in a number of public companies. He would, therefore, have a market for his stock and could receive a dividend income.

Even if the founder were able to attract sufficient stockholders to his private corporation he would create minority stockholders whose harassing potential might be more than he bargained for. If the company does poorly, the stockholders will be unhappy. If the company prospers, they will look for dividends or a public offering so that they might cash-out at a gain.

The majority stockholder may not want to go public because he would have to give too much of the company away. He may also object to such additional aspects of the public offering as the charge made by the underwriter, the cost of the prospectus, the expensive annual reports and the creation of many new backseat drivers who would limit his activities. Mr. Big would no longer be his own man.

As one can see, raising working capital through either a private or a public offering, assuming it can be accomplished, leaves a great deal to be desired.

Summary:

As things stand, public and private companies have about the same number of advantages and disadvantages with the disadvantages of each being the dominant characteristic.

The ESOT Adds A New Dimension To A Public Or A Private Company

"Going private" through an ESOT (or "going public internally") can provide the answer for greater stock price predictability. A private valuation of stock in connection with an ESOT relates directly to earnings and other measurable barometers of a corporation as opposed to having the price of stock remain dependent upon public emotion.

An ESOT can be the vehicle of "going private" or remaining private while having the advantages and essentially none of the disadvantages of being public. It can allow the founder to translate his unspendable capital into spendable cash with favorable consequences. An ESOT can infuse working capital into the company through the use of pre-tax dollars without going outside the company for investors.

> When the public places too low a valuation on the stock, the ESOT can buy stock in the public marketplace at the prevailing market price. The ESOT procures cash to make the purchase from the corporation. The contributions that the corporation makes to the ESOT would be deductible up to 15% or, in the broader definition, 25% of covered payroll limitations. In effect, the ESOT acquires stock of the company at a depressed price with dollars provided to a substantial degree by tax savings.

At such time as the stock appreciates, the company can have a secondary offering to gather in more capital in a favorable market climate.

4.

How To Increase Working Capital And Cash Flow Through An ESOT While Remaining Private

The company can create a tax-sheltered Employee Stock Ownership Trust into which the corporation may contribute annually and deduct from Federal and State income taxes an amount of stock or cash equal to 15% of participating employees' payroll, or possibly 25% if laminated with an appropriately designed money purchase plan as permitted under the 1974 Pension Reform Act.

If the company contributes newly issued stock to the Trust, the amount of taxes that would have been paid remains with the corporation. The resultant tax savings thereby increases the company's cash flow and working capital by an amount equal to the tax payment that would have been due had there been no such deduction.

> Any cash contribution that a corporation makes to an ESOT, a pension plan or a profit-sharing plan, generally reduces cash flow and working capital.

There is no compulsion on the part of either the corporation or its stockholders to sell stock to the ESOT, in which case the company can make cash contributions.

MODEL:

How A Corporation Can Increase Its Cash Flow And Working Capital Through An Employee Stock Ownership Trust

Assumption: $1 million covered payroll

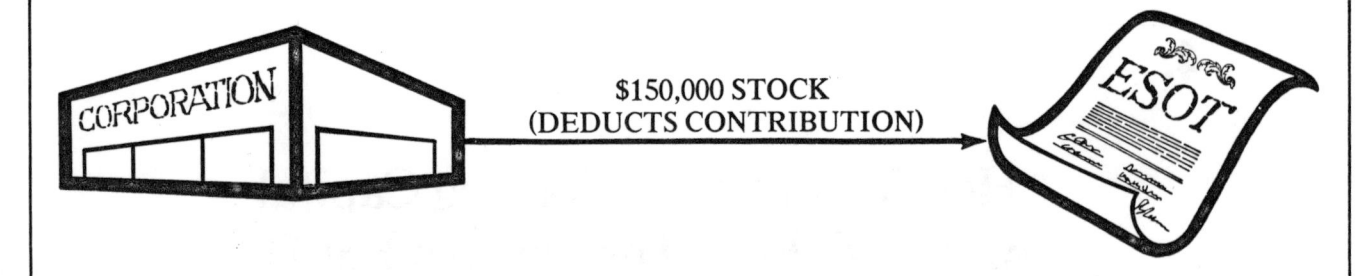

$150,000 STOCK
(DEDUCTS CONTRIBUTION)

—Corporation contributes stock to ESOT.
—Corporation deducts the contribution.
—Employee-participants are credited with shares in the Trust account.
—ESOT distributes shares of stock to retiring employees.

Summary:

Corporation receives tax deduction while making no cash outlay.
Corp, Inc., in the 54% combined Federal and State tax bracket saves $81,000 in taxes. (Tax rates vary by state.)
Cash flow and working capital is increased by amount of taxes saved.

HOW TO VALUE THE STOCK OF THE CORPORATION

The Public Company

The practical value of a public corporation is governed by what the public thinks the company's stock is worth. Supply and demand of the shares is a final price determinant. The public's judgment of the value of a corporation's stock may be affected by factors that are unrelated to the profitability of the company.

> All too often a buyer of securities bases his decision as to the price he will pay for stock on the amount he thinks someone else will pay for it sometime in the future. He may consider earnings and quality of management of secondary importance. His primary concern may be the multiple of earnings others might be willing to give for the stock.

This is double Russian Roulette. Not only must his crystal ball tell him the future earnings but it must also show the multiple of earnings the public will pay. If he is accurate on the first point but misjudges on the second he may lose heavily.

> During the early seventies there have been many public corporations whose stock sold for less than liquidation value or net worth. Thus the practical value was less than the true or absolute value.

The Privately Held Corporation

The value of a closely-held corporation may differ according to the purpose of valuation. Since the stock is closely-held, possibly within a family, or even wholly owned by one individual, there is no public marketplace, hence little need for determining a price for sale purposes—unless the owner wishes to sell the company.

Estate taxes provide a viable reason for fixing a value of the stock of a closely-held company. Upon the death of the stockholder, Uncle Sam assesses the value of the stock in the decedent's estate using a variety of methods or formula in arriving at the price per share.

Motivated by the urge to collect maximal taxes, the government often imputes a higher value to the stock than the price arrived at by the executor of the estate. There have been cases where the valuation for tax purposes has exceeded the recovery upon liquidation occasioned by the need to pay taxes. The existence of a Buy-Sell Agreement will go a substantial way toward fixing the value of the stock for estate tax purposes so long as it is on an arm's length basis, i.e., what a willing buyer will pay a willing seller, there being no compulsion to buy or sell on either one's part. A father-son agreement may not be considered arm's length while an agreement between two unrelated persons would tend to be considered so.

Valuing The Stock For ESOT Purposes

It is essential that a definite value be placed on the shares of the closely-held corporation that has implemented an Employee Stock Ownership Trust. There are two primary reasons for this:

1. It enables the corporation to determine the number of shares required to make up the allowable deductible contribution to the ESOT;
2. A definite value is needed to establish the number of shares to distribute to terminating or retiring ESOT participants.

Pricing Factors

The criteria that go to make up the price per share of a non-public company is varied. The hope is that the stock will be somewhat similar to that of a public company. Among the factors that are considered in determining the value of a share of closely-held company stock are:

1. Net worth;
2. Earnings record;
3. Transactions that have taken place in the sale of company stock;

4. Price earnings ratio of public companies of similar size that are in the same industry;
5. Earnings prospects for the near term future;
6. Stability of management;
7. Stability of the market for the company's product;
8. Stability of the company.

There are firms that specialize in evaluating stock of non-public companies. It is generally advisable to utilize the services of an independent company to determine the pricing of the stock. This will eliminate elements of wishful thinking or over-conservatism.

Accounting firms or underwriting departments of stock brokerage firms may be well qualified to value closely-held company stock. Some claim greater experience in evaluating service companies while others are more oriented toward those companies with greater inventory and equipment.

5.

How Stockholders Can "Cash-Out" While Still Retaining Control

Stockholders in closely-held companies, for all practical purposes, have no way of realizing cash for their stock during their lifetimes. They are prisoners of these non-liquid capital holdings which will ultimately be subject to erosion by estate and inheritance taxes.

If a stockholder sells some of his shares to the corporation, it is taxed as a dividend—essentially ordinary income. If he sells all of his stock to either an individual or a corporation, the cash he receives is taxed under the capital gains rules. He loses the company. There is little chance of anyone buying a minority interest in a closely-held corporation as we discussed earlier. If the individual did purchase some stock he would become a minority stockholder with harassing capability.

The answer... The stockholder sells some of his shares to the ESOT, using the cash for current enjoyment or personal investment diversification. This should be done with IRS approval so that the plan will remain for the exclusive benefit of the employees. The capital gains rules prevail. He retains sufficient shares to control the company (assuming he is majority stockholder). If he sells non-voting preferred or common stock there is no vote problem.

> If there is more than one major stockholder, it is readily apparent that one would not wish to sell so much of his stock as to upset the balance of control between the shareholders. In such a situation, the stockholders may each agree to sell that amount of stock which would permit retention of the present ratio of control while still enjoying the use of some cash.

The corporation contributes cash amounting to 15% of covered payroll, deducting the amount from taxable income.

End result ... Mr. Big got cash and capital gains treatment. Corp, Inc., received a deduction for providing the cash. Mr. Big still controls the company.

MODEL:

How Stockholder Can "Cash-Out"
Using Corporate Pre-Tax Dollars

Assumption: $1 million covered payroll.

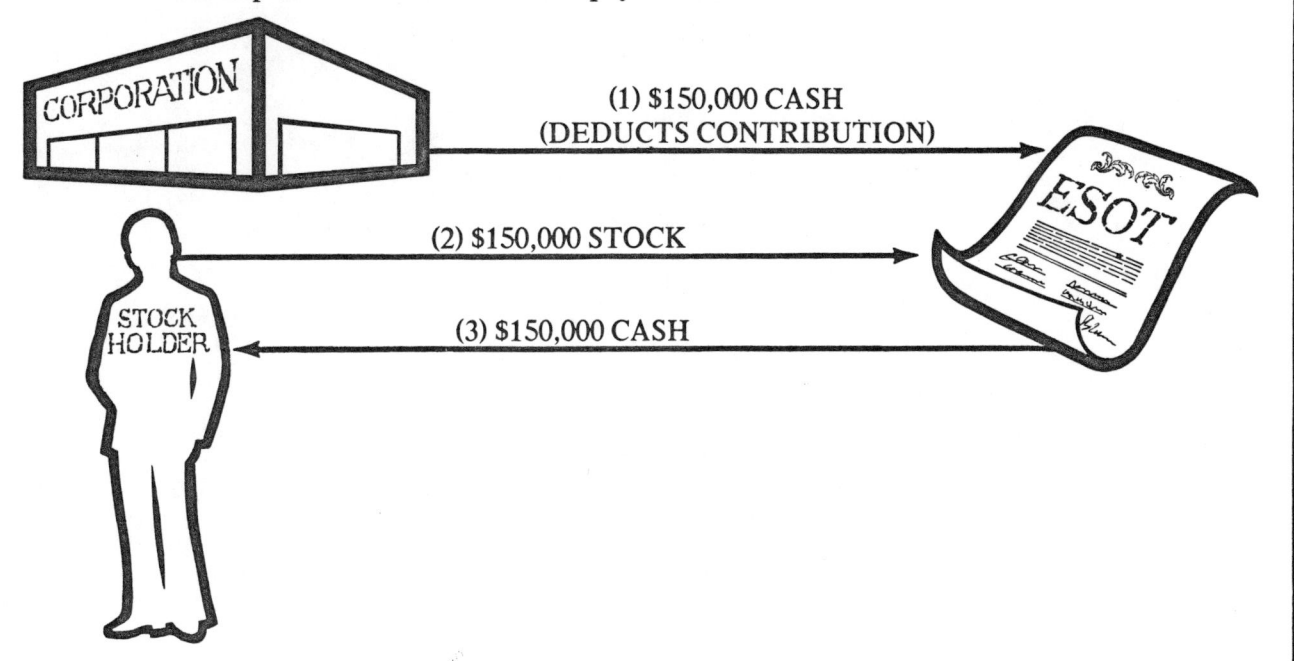

CORPORATION →(1) $150,000 CASH (DEDUCTS CONTRIBUTION)→ ESOT

STOCKHOLDER →(2) $150,000 STOCK→ ESOT

STOCKHOLDER ←(3) $150,000 CASH← ESOT

—Corporation contributes pre-tax cash to ESOT.
—ESOT uses the cash to purchase stockholder's shares of stock.

Summary:

Stockholder receives cash for his stock holdings which is tax-deductible by the corporation.

He receives capital gains tax treatment over the base.

6.

How The Corporation Can Repay Loan Principal And Interest With Pre-Tax Dollars

A corporation can build its new warehouse or refinance an existing loan at a cost of 46 cents on the dollar.

Here is how:

> The corporation sells shares valued at $500,000 to the ESOT which the Trust pledges at a bank in return for a $500,000 loan. The corporation stands behind the loan as guarantor. The ESOT pays the corporation $500,000 for the stock. The corporation then makes annual pre-tax cash contributions to the ESOT in an amount not exceeding 15% of its $1 million covered payroll, or $150,000, which it deducts from taxes.

The ESOT passes this on to the bank, thus servicing principal and interest. When the debt has been retired, the bank returns the collateralized stock to the ESOT.

> The employees have ownership in the shares to the extent of their participation in the Trust. The corporation has had the use of the borrowed funds and repaid its indebtedness—both principal and interest—with before-tax dollars.

Since the bank made the loan to the Trust rather than to the corporation, although the corporation guarantees the loan, the transaction can possibly be carried on the corporate books as a footnote rather than as a direct liability. There may be greater certainty as to the footnote result if, instead of guaranteeing the loan, the corporation merely guarantees to make cash contributions to the ESOT with which the Trust can service the debt.

MODEL:

How Corporation With No ESOT Repays Loan Principal And Interest

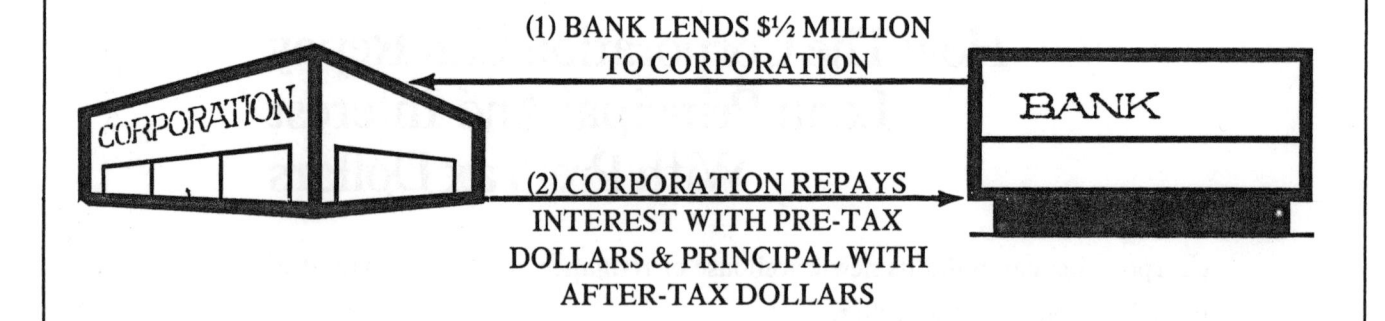

(1) BANK LENDS $½ MILLION TO CORPORATION

(2) CORPORATION REPAYS INTEREST WITH PRE-TAX DOLLARS & PRINCIPAL WITH AFTER-TAX DOLLARS

Summary:

Corporation in 54% combined tax bracket must earn $1,086,950 to repay $500,000 principal.

Corporation's cost for repaying each dollar of interest is 46 cents.

MODEL:

How Corporation With An ESOT Can Repay Loan Principal And Interest With Pre-Tax Dollars

Assumption: $1 million covered payroll.

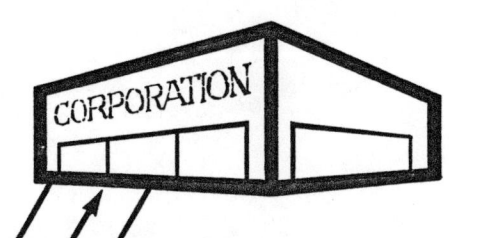

1. SELLS SHARES VALUED AT $½ MILLION
2. PLEDGES SHARES
4. PAYS $ ½ MILLION FOR STOCK
3. LENDS ESOT $½ MILLION
5. CONTRIBUTES AND DEDUCTS $150,000 CASH ANNUALLY (NET AFTER-TAX COST $69,000)
6. REPAYS ($150,000) PRINCIPAL & INTEREST
7. RETURNS STOCK WHEN DEBT IS RETIRED

Summary:

—Corp, Inc., requires money for expansion.
—Corp, Inc., sells shares of its stock to ESOT.
—ESOT pledges stock for bank loan.
—ESOT uses loan to pay Corp, Inc., for its stock.
—Corp, Inc., makes annual tax deductible cash contributions to ESOT in amounts up to 15% of covered payroll.
—ESOT repays bank loan as scheduled.
—Bank returns stock to trust when debt has been retired.

Summary:

Corporation repaid loan principal and interest with pre-tax dollars.
Net after-tax cost to repay each dollar of principal and interest is 46 cents.
Cost to pay $500,000 of principal is $230,000 plus after-tax cost of interest.

7.

How Corporations Can Make Acquisitions With Pre-Tax Dollars

Corporations that expand horizontally through the acquisitions route pay for the stock of the firm being acquired with cash, stock, or a combination of the two.

> Closely-held companies are seldom able to effect an acquisition through the use of stock due to a lack of marketability, in which case, after-tax dollars must be used.

The ESOT provides a means whereby the corporations can use pre-tax dollars to acquire another company.

Here is how it is done:

> The acquiring company makes a cash and/or stock contribution to the ESOT. This is deductible subject to the 15% of payroll rule. Additional financing, if needed, can come from a bank through the ESOT.

The ESOT pays the cash and/or stock to the stockholders of the company being acquired in exchange for that company's stock. The ESOT then exchanges this stock for an appropriate amount of the stock of the corporate sponsor of the ESOT. The acquiring corporation now owns the stock of the other corporation and its net worth has been increased by the value of that company. The acquisition was made with about 46 cents on the dollar.

MODEL:

How To Make An Acquisition With Pre-Tax Dollars

Assumption: $1 million covered payroll.

ACQUIRING CORPORATION—ABC, INC.   CORPORATION BEING ACQUIRED—XYZ, INC.

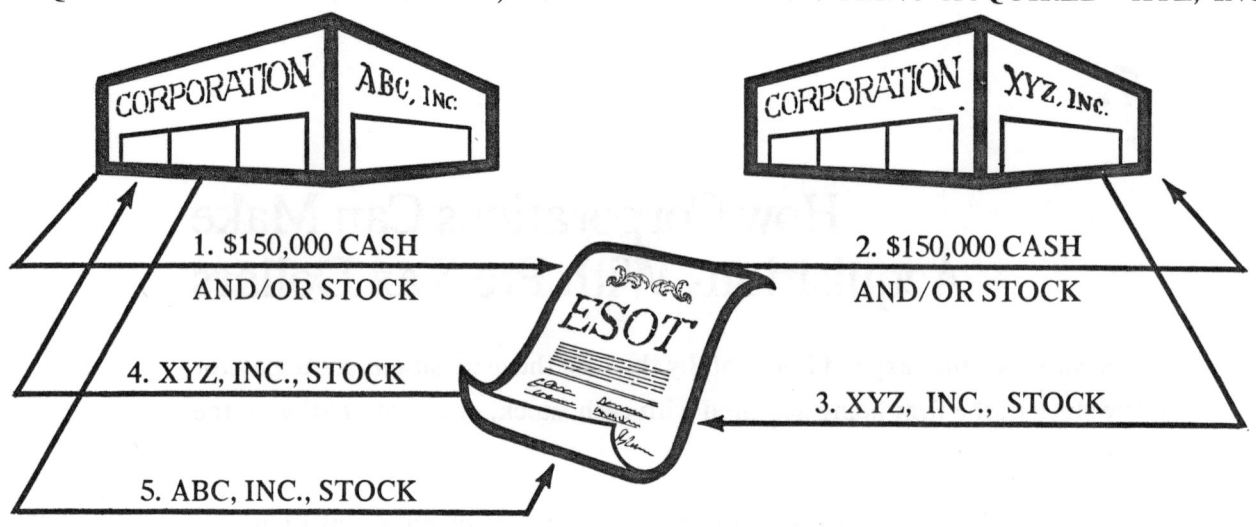

1. $150,000 CASH AND/OR STOCK

2. $150,000 CASH AND/OR STOCK

4. XYZ, INC., STOCK

3. XYZ, INC., STOCK

5. ABC, INC., STOCK

—Acquiring corporation, ABC, Inc., makes pre-tax cash and/or stock contribution to ESOT up to 15% of covered payroll.
—ESOT uses these funds and/or stock to purchase stock of XYZ, Inc.
—ESOT gives XYZ, Inc., stock to ABC, Inc., in exchange for ABC, Inc., stock.

Summary:

ABC, Inc., now owns XYZ, Inc., and its net worth is increased by the value of XYZ, Inc., accomplished with pre-tax dollars.

Employee-participants are credited with ABC, Inc., shares.

Additional financing if needed, can be accomplished with bank loan and can be repaid with pre-tax dollars.

Corporation with no ESOT must make acquisition with after-tax dollars.

8.

How To Have An ESOT, Profit-Sharing Plan, And A Pension Plan With No Net Cash Outlay

A corporation can have an ESOT in addition to a profit-sharing plan. However, the maximum deductible contribution it can make to the combination of plans is 15% of covered payroll. If there is a pension plan, a total of 25% can be contributed to the combination of plans.

Profit-Sharing Trusts are highly restrictive as to the investments they can own. As indicated earlier, the investments must qualify under the prudent man rule. A company's own stock may or may not be acceptable. An ESOT is unrestricted in this regard. The rationale is that the ESOT must make its distributions in the form of stock whereas the Profit-Sharing Trust makes cash distributions.

Various routes have been followed where there is an existing profit-sharing plan and management decides on the adoption of an ESOT. Here is one of the things that might be accomplished:

> The two plans can be operated in tandem. The corporation makes cash contributions to the Profit-Sharing Trust and stock contributions to the ESOT, the total contribution not to exceed 15% of participants' payroll.

An important difference between the two types of trusts is that a corporation can make contributions to a Profit-Sharing Trust only out of profits. A company can contribute stock to an Employee Stock Ownership Trust even in years wherein there is no profit, thereby creating losses to carry forward, or to carry back as the situation may permit. These losses might prove useful in future high earnings years.

Here is what happens when Corp, Inc., installs three plans:

> The company contributes, say 10% of participating payroll to an ESOT in the form of authorized but unissued stock, 5% to the Profit-Sharing Trust in the form of cash, and another 5% of participating payroll to a pension plan, a total, in this example, of 20% of covered payroll. The ESOT contribution requires no outlay of cash, yet the corporation gets a deduction.

Corp, Inc., with a covered payroll of $1 million, contributes authorized but unissued stock valued at 10% of covered payroll to the ESOT, viz., $100,000. The corporation, in the 54% Federal and State tax bracket, saves taxes amounting to 54% of $100,000, or $54,000. Since the $100,000 was in the form of authorized but unissued stock, not only is there no reduction in cash flow to achieve the $54,000 tax saving, but the cash flow actually increases by $54,000.

NOTE: The Employee Retirement Income Security Act of 1974 (ERISA) defines an Employee Stock Ownership Plan as, "... a qualified stock bonus plan or a stock bonus plan and a money purchase pension plan, both of which are qualified under Section 401 of the Internal Revenue Code of 1954, and which is designed to invest primarily in qualifying employer securities." The ESOP or its components must be individual account plans. If this definition involving the two plans is met, the company could contribute up to 25% of covered payroll in employer stock.

Money purchase pension plans or stock bonus plans which are not designed to be individual account plans would not be allowed to invest more than 10% of Trust assets in employer stock.

> A 5% of payroll, or $50,000, cash contribution to the Profit-Sharing Trust results in a $27,000 tax savings but reduces cash flow by $23,000. A $50,000 contribution into a pension Trust effects an equivalent tax savings and cash flow reduction. The reduction in cash flow occasioned by the contribution to the latter two Trusts is more than offset by the cash flow increase created by the ESOT. The net effect is a fringe benefit program comprised of an ESOT, a profit-sharing plan and a pension plan at no net cash outlay to the corporation!

MODEL:

HOW TO HAVE AN ESOT, A PROFIT-SHARING PLAN, AND A PENSION PLAN AT NO NET CORPORATE OUTLAY

Assumption: $1 million covered payroll.

Plan	Contribution % of Covered Payroll	Corporate Contribution	Tax Saving (A)	Increase (Decrease) In Cash Flow
ESOT	10%	$100,000 (B)	$ 54,000	$54,000
Profit-Sharing	5%	50,000 (C)	27,000	(23,000)
Pension	5%	50,000 (C)	27,000	(23,000)
TOTAL	20%	$200,000	$108,000	$ 8,000

(A) Assumes 54% Federal and State income tax bracket.
(B) $100,000 value of authorized but unissued stock.
(C) Cash contribution.

Summary:

> The corporation's cash flow increases by $8,000 after contributions to an ESOT, a Profit-Sharing Trust and a Pension Trust.

> The corporation creates an exceptional fringe benefit while reducing taxes by $108,000.

> Illustration assumes standard pension and profit-sharing plans whose purpose is to make cash rather than stock distributions to terminated participants.

9.

How It May Be Possible To Use Profit-Sharing Assets To Increase Corporate Working Capital

There have been numerous instances where a profit-sharing plan has been converted to an ESOT. The ESOT receives the profit-sharing Trust assets which are then used to purchase stock from the company. The proceeds increase the corporation's net worth and working capital.

> There is no taxable distribution since the assets of one tax-sheltered Trust go directly into another tax-sheltered Trust. The vesting rights of the profit-sharing participants is protected.

The employees should feel pleased if the corporation is a stable one that has generally experienced good earnings since they may now participate in the growth of the company that they spend their lives working for.

> Some District Directors of Internal Revenue Service have been more receptive than others in the implementation of this approach. An

alternative to this involves segregating the profit-sharing Trust's assets for the benefit of the participants, putting new contributions into the ESOT.

It is generally quite a simple matter to convert a profit-sharing plan to an Employee Stock Ownership Plan so long as it is accomplished in compliance with the I.R.S. Regs.

One amendment incorporated the following language:

WHEREAS, a profit-sharing plan was established by the Trustor, effective January 31, 1959; and,
WHEREAS, the Trustor desires to amend such plan to become an Employee Stock Ownership Plan;
NOW, THEREFORE, the Trustor agrees to the following:
1. Said plan is hereby amended by deleting said plan in its entirety and substituting in lieu thereof the following:
　　(Employee Stock Ownership Plan would follow.)

Examples of a plan and Trust are included in Chapters 38 and 39 of this book for the benefit of counsel.

MODEL:

Conversion Of A Profit-Sharing Trust To An ESOT
Using Assets To Increase Company Working Capital

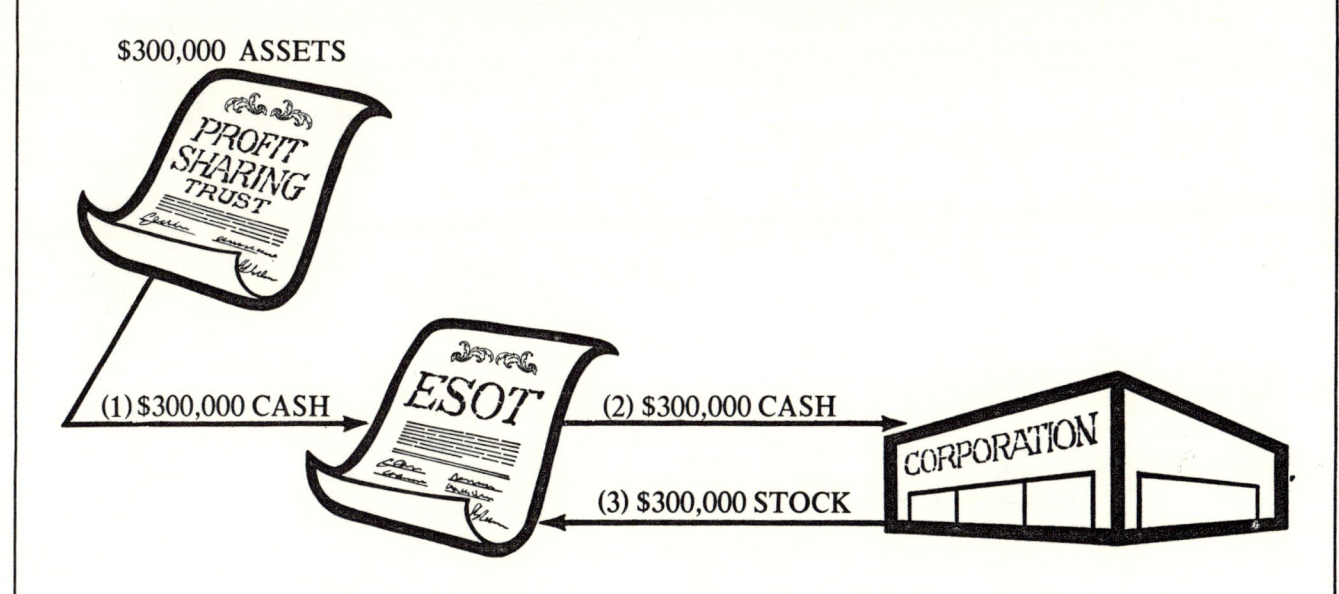

$300,000 ASSETS

(1) $300,000 CASH
(2) $300,000 CASH
(3) $300,000 STOCK

—Corporation has a profit-sharing Trust with assets of $300,000.
—It forms an Employee Stock Ownership Trust.
—Assets are converted from the profit-sharing Trust to the ESOT.
—Assets are liquidated and used to purchase stock of sponsoring corporation.
—Employee-participants retain vesting standing they had prior to the conversion.

Summary:

The corporation's cash flow, working capital and net worth is increased by $300,000.

The employees participate in the growth of their company.

10.

How It May Be Possible To Obtain A Refund Of Taxes Paid In Prior Years

The Internal Revenue Code allows corporate losses to be carried back three years and forward five years. However, losses must be carried back to the earliest point before they can be carried forward. Thus, a corporation is permitted, under certain circumstances, to obtain a tax refund for some or all of the Federal income taxes paid for the three prior years. Let's assume the corporation with a $1 million participating payroll installs an ESOT this year and makes a $150,000 contribution of stock or cash.

If the corporation had taxable income which totaled, coincidentally, $150,000 over the three years just preceding the current tax year and had paid Federal taxes aggregating $56,820 over the three-year period but broke even this year, the corporation could expect a tax refund of the $56,820 of taxes paid. The corporation created a loss of $150,000 by the contribution to the Trust, thus offsetting the taxable income. Since a loss can be carried back three years, the corporation gets its refund of taxes paid during that period.

MODEL:

How An ESOT May Make It Possible To Obtain A Tax Refund

Year	Taxable Income	Contribution To ESOT (Installed 1975)	Federal Taxes Paid
1972	$ 45,000	- 0 -	$15,100
1973	55,000	- 0 -	19,900
1974	50,000	- 0 -	17,500
SUB TOTALS	$150,000	- 0 -	$52,500
1975	- 0 - (A)	$150,000 (B)	($52,500) (C)

(A) Corporation broke even in 1975.

(B) Corporation installed an ESOT in 1975 to which it contributed 15% of payroll or $150,000 in cash or stock.

(C) Corporation is entitled by the Internal Revenue Code to a refund of Federal taxes paid for three preceding years because the ESOT contribution in 1975, a break-even year, offset the taxable income in those years. The refund in this model is $52,500.

11.

How To Transfer Stock After Death

A Buy-Sell Agreement is a useful planning tool for the proper disposition of a major shareholder's stock.

> Such an agreement is a written understanding between the stockholder and a second party. It is designed for the orderly transfer of his stock in the event of death or various other forms of cessation of active involvement in the business, including disability and retirement.

The two kinds of stock Buy-Sell Agreements most commonly used are the Cross-Purchase Agreement and the Stock Redemption Agreement.

> A Cross-Purchase Agreement governs the conditions under which stock will be acquired by surviving stockholders in the event of death of one of the stockholders.

A Stock Redemption Agreement covers the same contingency, the principal difference lying in the fact that the corporation, rather than an individual, buys the stock from the decedent's estate.

Where will the dollars come from to buy the stock when the stockholder dies? There are various ways of accomplishing the buy-out:

1. The surviving stockholders, or the corporation, as the case may be, can buy the stock from the executors with cash, notes, or a combination of the two. This must be accomplished with after-tax dollars. If the buyer is in the 50% tax bracket he must earn two dollars to pay one dollar for the stock. If the stock is valued at $100,000 the buyer must earn $200,000 to acquire the stock.

2. The potential buyer can pay for, own, and be the beneficiary of life insurance on the life of the stockholder whose stock is ultimately destined to be acquired. The premium is paid with after-tax dollars. The death proceeds are received by the beneficiary on a tax-free basis, providing the funds at the time they are needed, thus removing the burden of payment responsibility from the shoulders of the surviving stockholders and relieving the heirs of financial uncertainty. Instant liquidity for death taxes.

THERE IS ANOTHER WAY—THE FRISCH PLAN.

12.

The Frisch Plan— a way to fund an ESOT/Stockholder Buy-Sell Agreement or acquire ESOT Keyman Insurance with no net after-tax cash outlay

The Frisch Plan is an ideal method of providing liquidity to fund an ESOT/Stockholder Buy-Sell Agreement. It provides, at many ages, a means of insuring the stockholders who are party to the agreement at *no net after-tax cash outlay*. The agreement calls for the ESOT's having an option to buy stock from the deceased shareholder's estate and the executor of the estate selling at the valuation price that prevails when he dies. Paying for the insurance that enables the ESOT to buy the stock is where The Frisch Plan is applicable.

> Keyman insurance can also be purchased by the ESOT to compensate ESOT participants for the loss in value of their holdings occasioned by the death of a keyman.

Buy-Sell Agreements, to be worth their salt, should be funded. If the cash is not readily at hand when a stockholder dies, the agreement may not provide the security that was intended. The agreement would be mere lip service with no teeth in it.

> If the stockholder is insurable, there is no better way of funding the agreement than with life insurance on his life owned by the entity that will ultimately buy his stock. The other party to the agreement is usually another stockholder or the corporation itself.

As we are aware, the purchase of stock by individuals or corporations must be accomplished with after-tax dollars. The buyer in the 50% tax bracket must earn $200,000 to pay $100,000 to the seller.

> If insurance is used to provide liquidity for the agreement, the premiums are also paid with after-tax dollars if the insurance is owned by an individual or a corporation.

In funding a Buy-Sell Agreement—

—The Frisch Plan eliminates the need to pay premiums with after-tax dollars.
—The Frisch Plan negates the need for a reduction of cash flow or working capital in providing insurance.
—The Frisch Plan, believe it or not, often provides insurance at no net after-tax cash outlay to the corporation or to the stockholders.

Here is how The Frisch Plan works:
The ESOT/Stockholder Buy-Sell Agreement is funded by a policy insuring the life (lives) of the stockholder(s).

The ESOT is the owner, beneficiary and premium payor of the life insurance policy.

Where does the ESOT get the cash required to pay the premiums? From the corporation.

The Frisch Plan

Corporation to ESOT:

> The corporation makes cash contributions to the Trust in an amount equal to the annual premium. The contribution to the ESOT is income tax deductible so long as it does not exceed 15% of covered payroll. If the company is in the 54% effective Federal and State tax bracket, the contribution costs the corporation only 46 cents on the dollar.

ESOT to insurance company:

> Some of the cash which the corporation contributes to the ESOT is used by the ESOT to pay the premiums to the insurance company.

> A Whole Life policy is used. The ESOT, as owner of the policy, owns the cash value and dividends (assuming the insurance is a dividend-paying policy).

Insurance company to ESOT:

> In order to fulfill the stipulation of The Frisch Plan that there will be no net after-tax cash outlay for the insurance premiums, we will have the Trustee of the ESOT borrow from the policy an amount of cash sufficient to repay the corporation for its net after-tax outlay, by using those borrowed funds to purchase stock from the company.

Let's Work One Through:

> Assume the annual premium to be $5,000.

Corporation to ESOT:

> The corporation contributes $5,000 to the Trust. It deducts $5,000 from taxable income thereby saving approximately 54% in Federal and State income taxes, or $2,700.

> The company's cost at this point is, therefore, $2,300.

Insurance company to ESOT:

> The ESOT borrows $2,300 from the cash value of the policy assuming there is a cash value in the first year. (If there is no cash value the first year, the ESOT Trustee can borrow enough in the second year to pay the first two years' net Corporate outlays.)

ESOT to corporation:

> ESOT purchases $2,300 worth of newly issued (authorized but previously unissued company stock) from the company. This replenishes the corporation's cash flow and working capital. The net after-tax outlay that the corporation made to the Employee Stock Ownership Trust has now been repaid from the policy itself. *The net Corporate outlay zeros out.*

Second year:

> The ESOT must pay interest to the insurance company for the cash value it borrowed from the policy. In order to provide the Trust with cash, the corporation, as part of its regular 15% of covered payroll contribution, and in addition to its contribution covering the premium, also contributes to the ESOT an amount of cash sufficient to pay the interest.

ESOT to insurance company:

> The ESOT forwards the cash contribution equal to the premium and interest to the insurance company.

ESOT to corporation:

> The ESOT purchases stock from the corporation equal to the net after-tax corporate outlay for interest and premium. This replaces the lost working capital. The corporation is now whole again.

The Frisch Plan

The process is repeated annually.

The net corporate cash outlay for most ages is zero all the way past age 65—*no net after-tax cash outlay for insurance* in this illustration. Counsel should, of course, determine the feasibility of this or any other technique in this book, as well as the accuracy of any statement herein.

The charts on the following pages should help clarify the workings of The Frisch Plan.

THE FRISCH PLAN—HOW TO PURCHASE INSURANCE WITH NO NET AFTER-TAX CASH OUTLAY—THE BASICS

MALE, AGE 40

INITIAL FACE AMOUNT: $181,000   ANNUAL PREMIUM: $5,000

Year	(1) Premium	(2) Interest	(3) Total	(4) 46% of (3) After-Tax Cost to Corp.	(5) ESOT Pays to Ins. Co. Prem. & Int.	(6) Policy Cash Value	(7) ESOT Borrows Cash Val. From Policy & Buys Corp. Stock = to Col. (4)	(8) After-Tax Net Cash Outlay By Corp. (4)-(7)	(9) Cumul. Loan to ESOT From Policy Col. (4) Cumul.	(10) Net Cash Val. & Div. Reduced By Loan & Next Year's Int.*	(11) Net Death Benefit
1	$5,000	-0-	$5,000	$2,300	$5,000	$ 3,374	$2,300	-0-	$ 2,300	$ 937	$178,700
2	5,000	138	5,138	2,363	5,138	6,787	2,363	-0-	4,663	2,545	176,338
5	5,000	576	5,576	2,565	5,576	17,276	2,565	-0-	12,157	9,202	186,444
10	5,000	1,388	6,388	2,938	6,388	35,426	2,938	-0-	26,083	26,861	196,002
20	5,000	3,388	8,388	3,858	8,388	72,567	3,858	-0-	56,466	82,553	222,204
25 (Age 65)	5,000	4,690	9,690	4,457	9,690	90,478	4,457	-0-	82,617	109,540	233,782

(4) Assumes 54% effective Federal and State income tax bracket.

(9) Dividends are based upon current experience and are not guaranteed.
Some dividends have been used to purchase one-year Term insurance equal to the cash value.

Summary:

Average death benefit to age 65.....................$198,911.
Net cash accumulation (cash value and dividends)
in ESOT at age 65 after paying loan, interest,
and Term insurance..................................$109,540.*

By purchasing newly-issued stock from the company the ESOT replaces the firm's after-tax outlay. Net corporate outlay for any of the 25 years to age 65:   -0-.

*Net cash accumulation can be used by the ESOT for buying stock from the stockholders while they are still living.

This is not intended as tax advice. Any implication relative to tax consequences should be reviewed by one's own counsel. No aspect of this plan should be implemented other than under advice of counsel.

MODEL:

THE FRISCH PLAN
A Way To Fund A Stockholder-ESOT Stock Buy-Sell Agreement
Or Acquire ESOT Keyman Insurance With No Cash Outlay

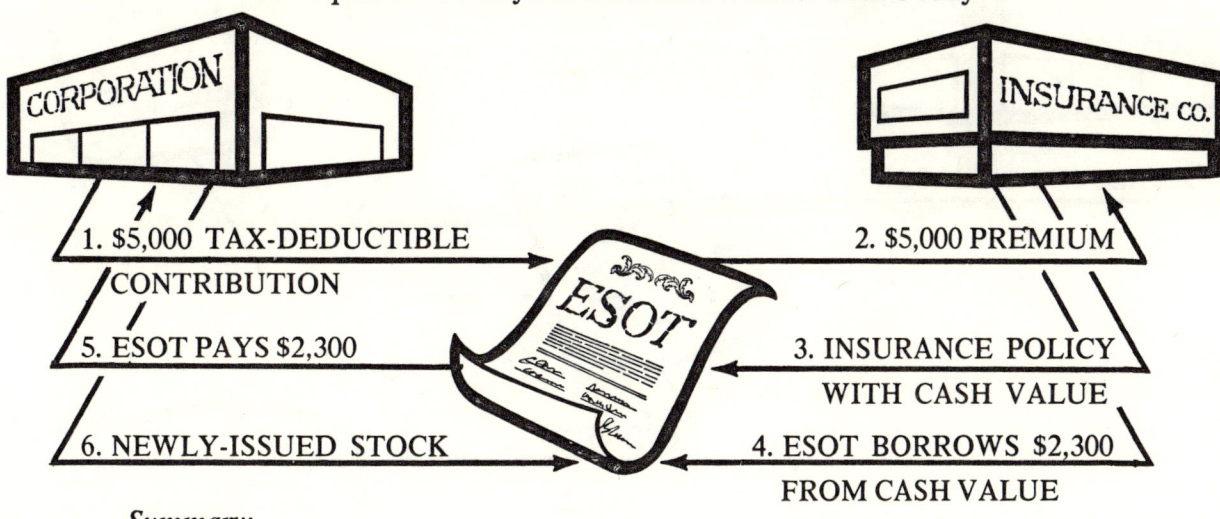

CORPORATION — **INSURANCE CO.**

1. $5,000 TAX-DEDUCTIBLE CONTRIBUTION
2. $5,000 PREMIUM
3. INSURANCE POLICY WITH CASH VALUE
4. ESOT BORROWS $2,300 FROM CASH VALUE
5. ESOT PAYS $2,300
6. NEWLY-ISSUED STOCK

Summary:

1. Corporation makes tax-deductible cash contribution to ESOT.

2. & 3. ESOT pays gross premium plus interest, if any, to insurance company for policy on the life of the stockholder. ESOT owns and is beneficiary of the policy.

4. ESOT borrows from the cash value an amount each year equal to the net after-tax corporate contribution ($2,300 in the example, assuming the 54% combined tax bracket). The ESOT must pay interest on the loan. The corporation's deductible contribution to the ESOT covers the premium and the interest, in addition to any contribution for other purposes.

5. & 6. The ESOT uses the borrowed cash value to purchase newly-issued stock from the corporation in an amount equal to the net after-tax cost to the corporation for its contribution to the ESOT. This replaces the net corporate outlay, thus replenishing the company's working capital and cash flow.

THE INSURANCE IS PURCHASED WITH NO NET AFTER-TAX CASH OUTLAY BY THE CORPORATION OR THE INSURED.

MODEL:

The Basic ESOT-Stockholder Buy-Sell Agreement

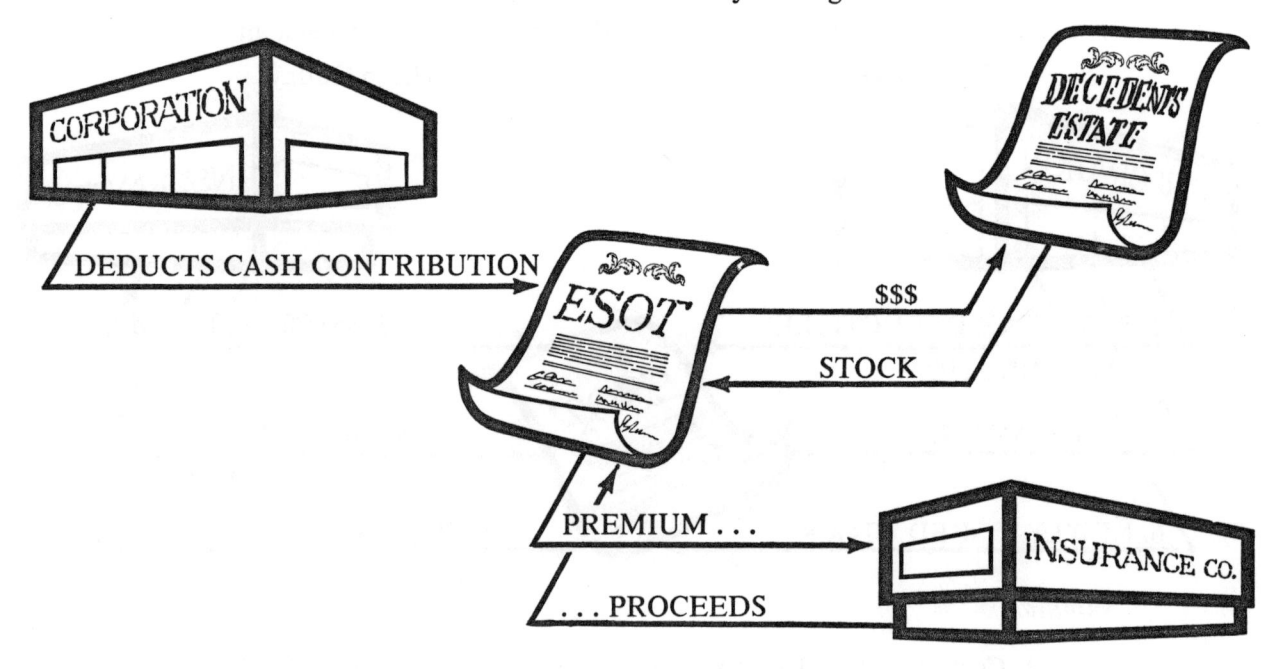

- ESOT and stockholder enter Buy-Sell Agreement.
- Corporation makes tax deductible stock and cash contribution to ESOT.
- ESOT purchases a life insurance policy on the stockholder's life. The ESOT is owner-beneficiary. Insurance is used to fund the Buy-Sell Agreement.
- Upon the stockholder's death, the insurance proceeds are paid to the Trust tax-free.
- The ESOT uses the proceeds to buy the decedent's stock from his estate in accordance with the agreement.
- The estate gets cash to pay Federal and State death taxes.

13.

The Stock Retirement Agreement Vs. The ESOT Buy-Out

It is quite easy for the would-be complete stock redemptions to be taxed unexpectedly as a dividend. This could occur if, after considering the amount of stock required to effect an IRC Section 303 redemption (for paying the taxes and administration costs occasioned by death) there is stock attributed to the decedent's estate that is not redeemed.

By the time a stockholder dies, it is possible that circumstances will have changed from those that existed at the time the stock retirement agreement was drafted. Changes in stockholdings among family members may have occurred which might have served the purposes of the relatives but could prove a disaster to the decedent's estate by causing the stock purchase to be taxed as a dividend. This would be the situation if the transaction were deemed not to be a complete redemption according to the rules.

Leaving some stock in trust for the stockholder's wife with his child as remainderman might prove the estate's undoing since the child's portion could revert to the mother, thus creating an attribution problem.

If a Buy-Sell Agreement is to have teeth, it is generally so worded that the owner of the stock is precluded from selling or gifting the stock during his lifetime without first offering it to the other party named in the agreement. The price cannot exceed a specified figure or formula. The estate of the decedent must be obligated to sell at that figure.

Assuming the price to be fair and arm's length in a stock redemption agreement, the proceeds will be considered merely a payment for the stock recovered by the corporation, rather than as a dividend.

It is important in drafting the agreement to consider the life insurance which is used for the funding. Unless the agreement excludes the insurance proceeds from the purchase price, part of the insurance proceeds proportionate to the stockholder's business interest would be included in the decedent's estate. A properly worded agreement can avoid this unfavorable treatment. The value of the stock would be included in his estate but the death proceeds of the insurance policy would not be.

Many areas for concern in the design and maintenance of a Stock Redemption Agreement can be minimized if an ESOT is installed. The ESOT could purchase a significant portion of the shareholder's stock during his lifetime. He makes a gift of the investments with the cash. The stock that remains in his estate can be the object of a Buy-Sell Agreement between the stockholder and the ESOT whereby the ESOT purchases the securities upon the shareholder's death. The ESOT could acquire the insurance using the outlay-free Frisch Plan. This technique should be used only upon advice of counsel.

There is no concern on anyone's part as to whether or not the redemption is complete bcause the corporation is not involved in the transaction.

The Employee Stock Ownership Plan once again proves its effectiveness as an estate planning device.

14.

The 303 Redemption Is Good— But ESOT May Be Far Better. Here's Why:

Section 303 of the IRC is often referred to as the "Bail Out" Provision of the Code. It is actually a means whereby the heirs of a stockholder of a corporation can get money out of the corporation tax-free—if the stockholder's estate qualifies for such tax treatment.

If it does qualify, stock can be redeemed (purchased) by the corporation in an amount that does not exceed the State and Federal death taxes, interest thereon, and the deductible administration and funeral costs of the estate, and the transaction will not be taxed as a dividend. It will merely be considered an exchange for stock because the basis of the stock is increased at the time of death so that there is little or no capital gains tax.

In order to become eligible for this tax advantage, the value of the stock of the corporation in question as determined for Federal estate tax purposes must be either:

(a) in excess of 35% of the gross estate; or
(b) more than 50% of the decedent's taxable estate.

If 75% or more of the value of the stock of two or more corporations is taxable in the gross estate, it is treated as the stock of a single corporation in determining whether the stock complies with (a) or (b) above. These are the primary provisions for eligibility for a Section 303 redemption.

Possible Pitfalls In Qualifying For 303:

> If the stockholder wishes to qualify for Section 303 he must plan on retaining the bulk of the stock so long as he lives. This precludes his cashing out a significant amount of stock during a period when he can enjoy the cash—namely, while he is alive.
>
> The ESOT would grant him the luxury of selling substantial blocks of stock to the ESOT without relinquishing control. Part of the cash could be given as a gift while some cash could be used to diversify his holdings. Still another portion of the cash could be used to buy insurance to pay the death duties.

It is also possible that the estate might not qualify for a 303 because of the stockholder's prowess in building other assets. Windfall stock profits coming just before he dies could prove a mixed blessing—great to have, but capable of messing up the 303!

> If a Section 303 redemption is to be made, the corporation must have adequate funds on hand. In order to do this the company must be very careful that it does not run afoul of Section 531 of the IRC, the provision dealing with unreasonable accumulation in surplus.

There is no problem if the accumulation is for the reasonable needs of the business. If it is determined that the accumulation is merely for the benefit of the estate of the deceased stockholder, the tax could be imposed. The penalty tax is 27½% on the first $100,000 of accumulation and 38½% on the excess above $100,000. This is over and above the basic corporate taxes. Thus, one is looking at taxes approximating 80% in the event of an accumulation violation.

The fine points involved in qualifying for Section 303 coupled with the simplicity of becoming a casualty of Section 531 causes one to give pause and ask—"Is there another way?"

Fortunately, there is—the ESOT.

Problems along these lines can be resolved if the corporation implements an ESOT. The Trust then buys some of the stock from the stockholder while he lives. He gets capital gains treatment and has the liquidity to pay estate costs. He also gains the opportunity of enjoying the use of the cash, thereby reducing his estate in the process.

A Buy-Sell could be arranged between the stockholder and the Trust for any remaining stock which he had not cashed out. The diversification of his holdings will enhance an equitable testamentary transfer to his heirs.

15.

How Large Stockholders In Public Corporations Can Sell Their Stock Without A Secondary Offering

A secondary offering can take two forms:

1. A founder can offer his stock simultaneously with the initial or primary corporate offering. It can be implemented on a basis whereby the sale is guaranteed by an underwriter in exchange for giving up some shares to him in addition to his fee. The underwriter must be confident of his ability to dispose of the stock on the open market. This offering can also be on a non-guaranteed basis which means that the seller has to take his chances that the stock will be sold.

2. The large stockholder-officer can offer his block of stock subsequent to the initial corporate offering. This is done via a prospectus which must be cleared with the Securities and Exchange Commission. The legal fees and other costs involved in the preparation are not insignificant. One must bare one's soul in the prospectus. Full disclosure is the keynote.

It may require several months to a year to have the prospectus cleared. By that time, the market climate may have changed considerably. The price of the stock may differ considerably from its price when the stockholder originally decided to sell.

Often the very act of offering stock precipitates a decline in the market value. Other stockholders may ask, "Why is Mr. Big selling? What does he know that I don't know?" He and others sell and the price declines.

The foregoing offers the large stockholders a less-than-ideal way to liquidate his stockholdings. In each case a severe loss of principal may result.

The ESOT Buys The Stock Privately

The large stockholder as well as the small ones can sell blocks of stock in varying size at periodic intervals to the ESOT, incurring no publicity or notoriety in the process. No prospectus is required, thus saving substantial dollars in legal fees.

Since no public announcement precedes the sale, the market value is unaffected. The ESOT must have cash in order to acquire the stock. The Trust can obtain cash by two means:

1. bank borrowings, to be repaid by pre-tax corporate contributions; or
2. pre-tax corporate cash contributions to the ESOT without the borrowings.

By selling stock to the ESOT, the shareholder can be more certain as to the price he will receive and the sale will not affect the value of anyone else's shares.

If he is the controlling stockholder he will undoubtedly control the Board which appoints the Administrative Committee that directs the Trustee as to how to vote the shares. The sale to the Trust will, therefore, have no practical effect upon his control of the firm so long as he retains a greater number of shares outside the ESOT than anyone else has.

16.

How Minority Stockholders Can Be Enticed To Sell Their Stock

Minority stockholders of publicly held corporations are part of the marketplace for the stock.

Minority stockholders in a privately or closely-held corporation can prove troublesome to the point of despair.

To become a minority stockholder in a public company, you simply go to your stockbroker and order some shares. You sell your stock in a similar manner.

You become a minority stockholder in a closely-held corporation in one of several ways:

1. you inherit the stock;
2. you are given the stock;
3. you buy the stock; or
4. you are one of the founders and are apportioned some stock.

A minority stockholder is in a bind. He has no final say as to how the business should be conducted. There is no way for him to salvage the value of the stock. If he expects dividends he is usually deluding himself. What then can he do? He might, because of his frustrations, elect to harass the majority stockholder in the hope of eliciting a dividend payment or getting the major stockholder to buy him out at a fair price.

It is quite common for a well-meaning parent, in trying to be fair to all of his children, to Will his closely-held founder's stock to each of them, whether or not they are involved in the business. The son who devotes his waking hours to the corporation might learn to resent building a company for his stockholder sister who contributes no effort to the growth of the firm. The sister may resent not receiving a share of the profits. The father may have been better advised to leave the whole business to the son, giving him a free reign to build it properly. In giving the daughter her choice, he could Will other property to her or make her beneficiary of a life insurance policy.

> Assuming the minority stockholder does exist, the ESOT could serve to buy the stock at its current valuation. In so doing, the minority stockholder would receive cash for the stock and capital gains treatment as well. The majority stockholder could be his own man in running the business.

The ESOT purchases the stock with dollars that were contributed by the corporation and which the company deducted. The ESOT can be effective in breaking up potential voting blocks by enticing one or more in the group to sell out. This pre-tax technique is obviously preferable to one requiring after-tax dollars.

How To Transfer The Business To Heirs Or Employees Through The ESOT

> Competent second-line management is essential to the continuity of a business enterprise. If present management desires that the business be carried on after his death, retirement or disability, he faces two choices. He may:
>
> 1. sell the company to those who would provide management or merge with them; or,
> 2. develop second-line management.

Selling the company at full value must be accomplished while management responsible for the firm's success is still functioning effectively. A sale, as a rule, precludes participation in future profits. Thus, selling a firm even under optimum conditions while the controlling stockholder-executive is in his pre-retirement years occasions a guaranteed loss of benefits from future corporate growth to that stockholder. It also deprives him of his chosen activity.

Selling the company, then, is not a panacea. Second-line management can be more profitable to the controlling stockholder-executive since he could continue to benefit from the company's ongoing profits. He could have reasonable assurance that the firm would continue to function in the event of his disability, retirement or death.

> In order for the second-line team to have the incentive to remain with the corporation the key people should be given a stake in its capital ownership.

The ESOT can provide the opportunity for such proprietorship. Those in the executive category would tend to constitute the more highly compensated group who would, in turn, be credited with a larger share of the allocations to the ESOT.

> This provides an incentive for tenure in the event of the incapacity or demise of the founder.

17.

How To Remove Assets From The Estate —Private Annuity Or ESOT?

The eroding effects of Federal estate taxes, State inheritance taxes, administration and probate costs when an individual dies can be minimized by a variety of planning techniques. These techniques serve to remove assets from the estate, thereby reducing taxes and other costs of dying.

One such technique is the private annuity or installment buy-out. This vehicle is used most commonly in a father-son situation where the father owns an asset such as a business or a piece of income property that he would like to pass on to his son in a manner that would preclude its being taxed in the father's estate.

The father transfers ownership of the company stock to the son in exchange for a lifetime income, calculated on the basis of a government annuity table. The son pays his father an income for life. Part of each installment would be considered return of capital on which there is no tax; part is taxed as capital gains; and the balance is ordinary income.

The father must retain no incidence of ownership if the asset is to be considered to be excluded from his estate. The son's promise to pay must be unsecured. It is for this reason that the parties to the agreement must be very close—such as parent and offspring.

> It is possible for the son to pay a greater amount ultimately through the private annuity method than he would have paid in an outright purchase. This could occur if the father should outlive his expectancy, as determined by the government table alluded to earlier. The son would still be obligated to make the stipulated payments. The installments that the father receives beyond his expectancy would be taxed as ordinary income.

In the event the son predeceases his father, the son's payments to the father would be an obligation of the son's estate. The father could be made the beneficiary of insurance on his son's life to assure the value of the obligation. Since the son's estate would still be obligated if insurance proceeds were paid to the father directly, the son could make his own estate or a Trust beneficiary so that the liquidity would be available to pay his father. The father could insure his own life to cover the difference between the amount he receives and the value of the transferred property.

> A serious problem may arise if the transferred property is the father's control stock of his closely-held company. Once he transfers ownership of the company stock it is gone forever. If he still intends to control the firm during his remaining years or changes his mind about not desiring further involvement, the private annuity may not serve his best interest.

> It should also be noted that the son purchases the asset with after-tax dollars.

The ESOT Method

An ESOT, on the other hand, may fulfill his objectives. The ESOT route would permit him to cash out to the extent desired while still retaining sufficient shares to assure continuing control for so long as he wishes.

The father could gift or Will some shares to the son and enter a Buy-Sell Agreement with the ESOT, funded by insurance.

Result: The son becomes the largest stockholder, other than the father. The father gets cash to enjoy during his lifetime, taxed as capital gains. He can diversify his estate holdings or give gifts to his other children without their becoming involved in the business in which they may not be interested.

The program of giving serves to reduce his estate and his potential liability. The funded Buy-Sell Agreement through the ESOT provides liquidity with which his executors can pay estate tax liability and other costs. The insurance for funding the agreement is purchased with pre-tax corporate dollars that were contributed to the Employee Stock Ownership Trust, as opposed to the private annuity method whereby the son makes the purchases with after-tax dollars.

18.

How ESOT's Can Help Franchisors And Franchisees

A characteristic attributable to all franchisors at one time or another is the desire to expand horizontally with minimal cash expenditure. In accomplishing this end, franchisors use the tried and true growth mechanism, the O.P.M. (Other People's Money) method.

The franchisor develops an idea, a uniform system, controls on supplies, and a training program. He entices prospective franchisees to contribute capital and a percentage of gross income on the basis of a pro-forma which suggests the likelihood of a profit-laden future, which in many instances does indeed occur.

Frequently franchisees don't have enough cash to buy enough inventory to realize maximum sales potential. This maintains a lid on profitability for both the franchisees and the franchisors.

New automobile dealerships represent a form of franchise that requires a large capital outlay for inventory. The more successful car dealerships maintain a substantial and burdensome payroll as well.

> The proper use of an ESOT can help provide needed working capital to dealers which should enhance their net profits if the capital is employed wisely.

A dealer could contribute newly-issued stock to an Employee Stock Ownership Trust that the franchisee implements. By contributing authorized but unissued stock to the Trust, the corporation gets a tax deduction resulting in increased cash flow because of the tax savings.

The additional cash flow can be used to increase inventory which in turn means greater profits. All other factors remaining constant, if profits increase sufficiently to improve earnings per share, the stockholders and the participants of the ESOT will experience a growth in the value of each share of stock in which they have a beneficial interest. This annual growth can result in a significant deferred compensation benefit for the ESOT participants.

Since automobile dealerships require so much capital, they would find the leveraging capability of an ESOT very useful. The dealership could acquire inventory at about half price, thereby increasing its profit margin substantially.

The dealership's ESOT could borrow money which it would repay through future corporate cash contributions. The corporation would deduct the contribution to the Trust. Uncle Sam, therefore, contributes about 54% toward repayment of the ESOT's indebtedness—both principal and interest. Not a bad way to acquire inventory—the U.S.M. (Uncle Sam's Money) approach.

This could be just the answer for an auto dealership's leasing operation. Auto leasing works on a fairly narrow profit margin.

> If the dealership could acquire some of the cars it leases at half the cost its competitors must pay, it could place itself in a most competitive position. This can be accomplished through the leverage

afforded by the creative use of an Employee Stock Ownership Trust.

If the dealership has had a profit-sharing plan, the corporation can apply to the Internal Revenue Service to have it converted to an ESOT. Assuming IRS grants approval, the assets that the profit-sharing plan had can, with IRS approval, be liquidated and used by the Employee Stock Ownership Trust to buy corporation stock. The participants of the profit-sharing Trust maintain their same vested position in the ESOT. The shares of dealership stock that the ESOT purchases are apportioned among the ESOT participants' accounts.

> The profit-sharing assets had been out of the corporation's reach but they now provide much-needed working capital which will enable the dealership to buy cars to sell or lease.

> The most logical source of funds for the purchase would come from life insurance which the ESOT buys on the stockholder's life. The premium dollars are derived from pre-tax dollars contributed by the company.

> The Bank Trustee will not, therefore, find itself in a position as liquidating Trustee of the business in order to pay the taxes. The Trust would gain immediate liquidity from the insurance proceeds. The employees would benefit as participants in the ESOT. The bank would maintain an available corporate customer that it would have lost had it become necessary to sell the company for liquidity.

> The other stockholders, if any, would be delighted to find their company still intact even though the major stockholder had died. The estate would probably pay much less in taxes because the arm's length Buy-Sell Agreement and the independent appraisal of the corporate stock, would tend to peg the value of the stock for estate tax purposes.

The Bank's Role In Preserving The Value Of A Thinly-Held Company

When a bank is Trustee of an estate in which there are large holdings of stock in a thinly-held corporation it is in a tenuous position. If the bank offers the stock for sale, this very act would undoubtedly depress the stock's value.

If the Trustee doesn't sell, there may not be sufficient liquidity to pay estate and inheritance taxes and probate expenses.

The solution could be identical to that outlined in connection with the closely-held corporation—namely, the implementation of an ESOT to provide a marketplace for the stock.

> The Trust should own key man insurance on the life of the key profitmaker(s) to assure the participants the value that would otherwise be lost if the key profitmaker(s) died. The insurance is acquired with pre-tax corporate cash contributions.

The ESOT should also enter into a funded Buy-Sell Agreement with the major stockholders for reasons outlined in Chapters 11, 12, and 13.

> Factors relating to automobile dealerships add complications which may not be applicable to other forms of dealerships or franchises.

For example, the big automobile manufacturers generally demand the right to approve of stockholders in a franchise. A large California automobile dealership, whose franchise is with one of the big three manufacturers, was given such approval by the manufacturer after certain restrictions on the stock were imposed through the ESOT. The plan was also granted a favorable IRS Letter of Determination.

> Before implementing an ESOT it would be wise to contact the Department of Motor Vehicles of the state wherein the ESOT is domiciled to be certain there is no licensing problem in connection with the Trust.

19.

How To Get Personal And Corporate Tax Deductions That Exceed The Value Of Your Gift

An ESOT can help you help your college, hospital, church, other favorite charitable organizations, and yourself.

If you are a stockholder you can donate shares of your appreciated stock to a qualified public charity and get a tax deduction equaling the current value of the gift. If you have held your appreciated stock sufficiently long for it to be considered long-term gain property (six months is the rule at the time of this writing), your limit for the deduction is 30% of your adjusted gross income. Excess amounts can be carried over five years. You need pay no capital gains tax on the appreciation over the base cost of the stock. The gift also serves to reduce your taxable estate.

If the security that is gifted to the charitable institution is publicly-traded stock, the donee, such as a college, sells it in the open market to reduce the gift to usable cash. If the stock in thinly traded it may be difficult for the donee to sell a significant block of stock without affecting the stock's price adversely.

A donation of a minority interest in a non-public company is all but useless to a charitable organization, since there is no market for the stock. The charity needs cash—not just a vote as a minority stockholder.

> The gift of stock may be made in such a way that it is essentially the equivalent of cash. Let us assume the donor to be the controlling stockholder in a closely-held non-public corporation that installs an Employee Stock Ownership Trust. He gives some of his personally-owned stock to his favorite university, a qualified public charity under the Internal Revenue Code. This entitles the donor to an income tax deduction equal to the gift. If he limits the gift to 30% of his adjusted gross income he pays no capital gains tax on any appreciation in the value above his basic price.

The university, thereafter, may sell the stock to the ESOT, a logical marketplace for the stock. The ESOT pays the university an amount of cash equal to the appraised value of the securities. It is assumed here that no collusion is involved in the transaction.

The ESOT could obtain the liquidity for the purchase from corporate cash contributions not to exceed 15% of covered payroll. The corporation would deduct these contributions from taxable income. The company's board of directors, of which the donor is chairman and a major corporate stockholder, still retains control, to the extent that the board appoints the Administrative Committee of the ESOT that directs the Trustee who votes the shares purchased by the Trust. All are subject to responsibilities of prudency.

Tax Effect On The Donor

The donor receives an income tax deduction for the current value of the gift. Though the gifted stock may have cost him only $2,000, if it is currently valued at $10,000, he is entitled to a $10,000 income tax deduction.

If he is in the 50% Federal tax bracket he saves $5,000 in income tax.

Personal/Corp. Deductions That Exceed Value Of Your Gift 83

His estate tax is also reduced by having removed the asset from his estate.

Tax Effect On The Corporation

The corporation contributes $10,000 of cash to the ESOT, thus providing the liquidity with which the Trust can pay for the shares. If the company is in the 54% Federal and State combined tax bracket, it saves $5,400 in taxes.

Summary:

>The combined income tax deduction is 200% of the value of the gift.
>The combined income tax savings is 104% of the gift.
>The estate tax savings, assuming donor is in the 50% estate tax bracket, is $5,000.
>The public charity gets $10,000 worth of stock which it can sell to the ESOT for $10,000 in cash.

MODEL:

How To Get Personal And Corporation Tax Deductions That Exceed The Value Of Your Gift To An IRS Qualified Public Charity

- Donor gives public or private corporation stock, which he owns, to a qualified public charity. Value of stock is $10,000.
- Corporation whose stock is gifted has an ESOT to which charity sells its stock.
- Corporation contributes $10,000 in cash to ESOT which corporation deducts from taxable income.

Income Tax Deductions:

DONOR'S DEDUCTION	
(For contribution to charity)	$10,000
CORPORATION'S DEDUCTION	
(For contribution to ESOT)	10,000
TOTAL DEDUCTIONS	$20,000

NOTE: Donor reduces gross estate by $10,000.
Estate tax savings: $5,000 (50% estate tax bracket).

Income Tax Savings:

DONOR (50% bracket)	$ 5,000
CORPORATION (54% bracket)	5,400
COMBINED INCOME TAX SAVINGS	$10,400

Summary:

Value of gift	$10,000
Total deductions	20,000
Total income tax savings	10,400
Estate tax savings	5,000
Donor's current cash outlay	ZERO
Corporation's cash outlay	$10,000

20.

How A Corporation Can Facilitate A Divestiture With An ESOT

Companies may wish to divest themselves of subsidiaries for a variety of reasons:

> Corporations are sometimes ordered to make a divestiture because of an anti-trust ruling;

> An operating unit might not fit synergistically with the other units or divisions of a company; or

> A unit might be a financial loser.

A divestiture can be as simple or as complex as the parties wish to make it. Part of the consideration, for example, might be in the form of a subordinated note taken by the company doing the divesting, covering a sale and leaseback arrangement.

More specifically, the corporation can divest itself of a subsidiary by selling its physical assets. It then leases the assets back, taking a subordinated note from the buyer for all or a portion of the purchase price.

A cash purchase for the unit involves after-tax dollars. An individual or a corporation buying the unit, must repay the bank loan, if one is involved, and gets a deduction for interest but not for principal.

The ESOT can provide an interesting method of letting the buyer accomplish the acquisition with pre-tax dollars, thereby making it more logical for him to go through with the deal.

Here is how it is done:

Original, Inc., decides to divest itself of a profitable unit with its management, manpower, machinery and customer list intact. A new corporation, Unit, Inc., is formed into which the assets and personnel are transferred. Unit, Inc., in turn adopts an Employee Stock Ownership Trust. Original, Inc., sells Unit, Inc.'s stock to the ESOT. The Trust pays for the stock by borrowing from a bank. The loan is backed by the assets of the new company, which starts out as a profitable going concern.

The employees are all participants.

The new corporation makes pre-tax cash contributions to the ESOT amounting to 15% of covered payroll.

The ESOT liquidates the loan which was really paid by the corporation with 46 cent dollars. The employees, benefiting in the form of participating shares of the Trust feel a pride of ownership. They are building equity which will not be taxable until shares of the stock are distributed to them, probably at retirement.

The president of the new corporation may have purchased a relatively small number of shares from the original corporation with out-of-pocket after-tax dollars. This assures him immediate control of the new company. The board of directors appoints the administrative committee which, of course, votes the proxies for the stock.

MODEL:

Divestiture Through An ESOT

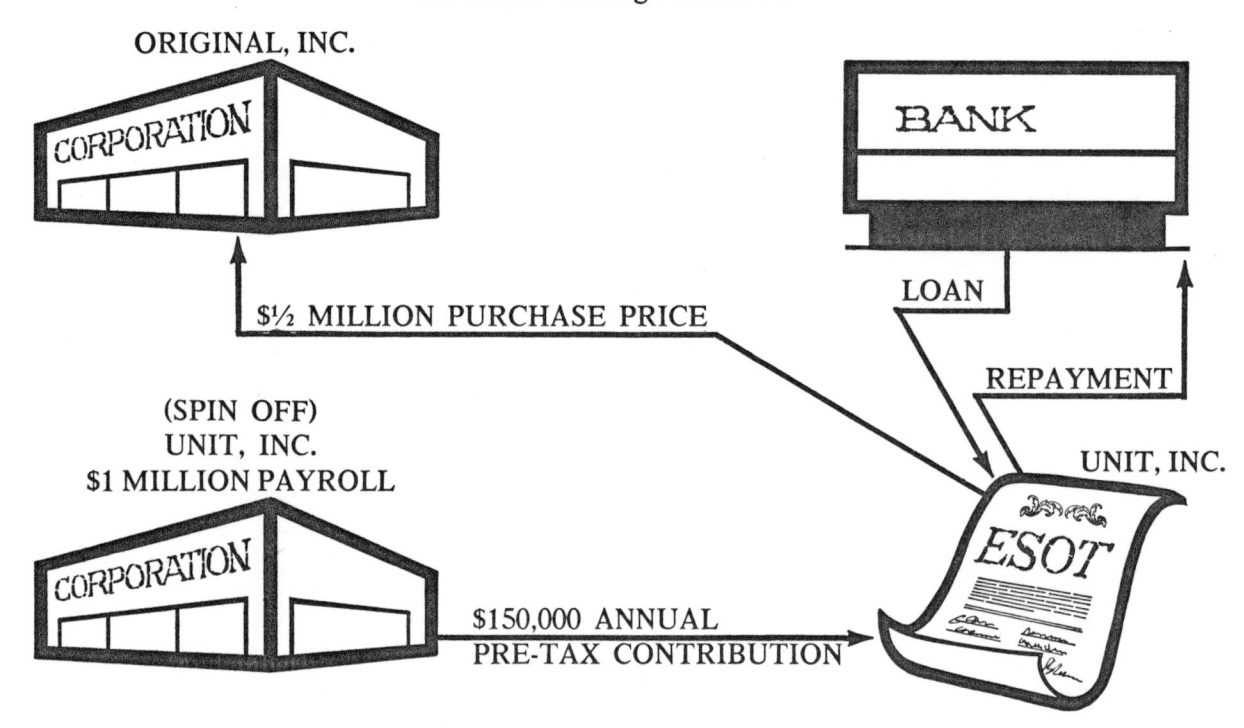

ORIGINAL, INC.

$½ MILLION PURCHASE PRICE

BANK

LOAN

REPAYMENT

(SPIN OFF)
UNIT, INC.
$1 MILLION PAYROLL

UNIT, INC.
ESOT

$150,000 ANNUAL PRE-TAX CONTRIBUTION

—Original, Inc., wishes to divest itself of a profitable operating unit valued at $½ million.
—It forms a new corporation, Unit, Inc., into which all assets and personnel are transferred.
—Unit, Inc., is a profitable going concern with a $1 million payroll.
—Unit, Inc., forms an ESOT.
—Original, Inc., sells the stock of Unit, Inc., to the ESOT.
—ESOT borrows $½ million from bank so as to buy Unit, Inc.'s stock from Original, Inc.
—ESOT puts up stock as collateral for bank loan.
—Unit, Inc., makes pre-tax deferred compensation cash contributions to ESOT amounting to 15% of payroll, or $150,000, annually.
—ESOT uses annual contributions to service debt.
—Bank returns stock to ESOT as loan is retired.
—Employees own shares of the ESOT which owns the stock of Unit, Inc.
—Employees are not taxed until stock is distributed, generally at retirement.
—The divestiture was made easier by making it possible for the purchaser to acquire the company with pre-tax dollars.

21.

How A Corporation Can Help Avoid A Takeover

Many public corporations are ripe for a takeover. Their stock is selling at bargain basement prices. Some of these companies might wish to buy some of their stock on the open market. This requires cash.

> Though the corporation might enjoy a good cash flow, its cash reserve may be inadequate to purchase meaningful amounts of stock from the public. Resourceful management might resort to an ESOT for the answer.

One corporation let its Employee Stock Ownership Trust tender for many thousands of shares of its stock. In order to procure the funds required for the acquisition of the shares, a bank loan was negotiated whereby the Trust borrowed the necessary funds from the corporation which, in turn, borrowed from a bank.

> The corporation has been making pre-tax cash contributions to the

Trust with which the ESOT uses to repay its indebtedness to the corporation.

A possible step for the future was to arrange for long-term financing to enable the corporation to liquidate the shorter-term note.

An extract from Schedule 13D describing the E-Systems, Inc., Employee Stock Ownership Trust's tender offer follows on the next page.

Extract from
SCHEDULE 13D

Filed pursuant to Rule 14d-1
under the Securities Exchange Act of 1934

by

E-SYSTEMS, INC.
EMPLOYEE STOCK OWNERSHIP TRUST

July 17, 1973

Item 4. Purpose of Transaction.

The purpose of the Plan is to assist employees over the course of their years of employment with the Company to accumulate capital ownership in the Company in order to provide economic security and independent income for such employees upon their retirement. The Plan is a continuation of two savings and investment plans which were originally established by the Company in 1967 and 1969, and the rights and privileges of the employees participating in those plans have been preserved under the Plan. Employee participation in the savings and investment plans was voluntary and required deductions from the employees' pay. Because the Plan does not require employee contributions and includes all full-time employees of the Company, the Company's management believes that the Plan will provide more incentive for all the Company's employees to increase their efforts on behalf of the Company.

The Plan is a stock bonus plan which permits all full-time employees to become beneficial owners of an interest in the Company which vests over a period of years of service, building capital ownership among all the employees. By thus closely linking capital ownership with day-to-day performance of work by all employees, it is the opinion of the Company's management that productivity will be enhanced and employee turnover will be reduced, thereby benefiting all owners of the Company's securities. The Company expects that such productivity increases should more than offset the cost of the Plan, although neither the Trust nor the Company can represent or warrant that such results will be achieved.

The purpose of the tender offer is to provide the Trust initially with a sufficient number of shares of the Common Stock at a price which the Trust believes to be favorable in order to expand the limited scope of the savings and investment plans by permitting participation in the Plan by all employees of the Company, and thereby furnishing such employees with an ownership basis in the Company sufficient to accomplish the purposes of the Plan.

22.

How A Public Company Can Go Private

A company can be considered to be a public company if it has offered its stock for sale to the public and the public has responded favorably so as to own an adequate percentage of the corporation. A company's stock that is just being offered to the public for the first time is called a "new issue" and is traded on the Over The Counter market (OTC) thereby falling under the regulatory jurisdiction of the National Association of Security Dealers.

> In the event the stock is held in round lots (100 shares) by a sufficient number of different shareowners and the corporation meets certain standards, the company can apply for listing on the American Stock Exchange (AMEX) or on the New York Stock Exchange (NYSE).

A public corporation attempting to go private is monitored rigidly by the SEC. It must disclose to the public its financials as well as its reasons for wanting to go private. The procedure must be devoid of manipulation or any of the machinations of fraud.

> A company can tender for its own shares, i.e., offer to buy them back from the public, or it might offer a convertible debenture which is convertible into non-voting stock. Both forms of repurchase are with after-tax dollars.

The compensation of the underwriters who took the company public often includes a block of the company's stock. The founders can be expected to retain majority control and the balance of the stock goes out to the public. The proceeds of the sale adds to the corporation's working capital.

> From that moment on, the Las Vegas syndrome comes into play. The stock purchased by outsiders is traded in the public marketplace. Those who bought at offering price may, with good fortune, sell at a profit or they may suffer a substantial loss. In either event, the corporation got its working capital and should not have to be overly concerned about the fluctuations in the marketplace. Those who control the company would like to see the stock develop a good track record so that it can go out to the public for more money later on in the event it requires additional capital.

The founders do worry since their future security is tied to the price of the stock at such time as they wish to sell it. They dream of cashing out someday —hopefully at a handsome multiple.

> Founders can hope to sell through a secondary offering which can be frightfully expensive and there is not always assurance of success. As mentioned earlier, there is a possibility of the public's misinterpreting the motives of the seller in a secondary and the other stockholders start to unload, thereby depressing the stock.

"Going private" would normally require that the corporation repurchase the stock from stockholders reducing the number of shareholders to a point at which the stock is no longer considered to be a public stock. This definition varies with the exchange on which the stock has been traded as well as by state requirement.

> The regulations of the NYSE, for example, provide that in order that a company's stock remain listed, more than 600,000 shares must be in public hands and of these shares a minimum of 1,200 shareholders must hold round lots.

The Securities and Exchange Commission has its own rules regarding a multitudinous array of filings and reportings. It exempts a firm from the major portion of these requirements if the number of outside stockholders declines to fewer than 300.

> In tendering for its own stock the corporation must offer top dollar. It must also effect the purchase with after-tax dollars. If the tender offer is a success and the public market is eliminated, the price of the stock can thereafter be determined by an independent appraisal or by agreements, if indeed there is a need.

There is one major flaw in this approach. Without a public marketplace, who do the remaining stockholders sell to unless they plan on selling the company. Here is where the ESOT solves the problem. The corporation installs an ESOT. The ESOT, not the corporation, makes a tender offer for the stock. It can afford to be more generous in offering price than if the corporation tendered because it uses pre-tax dollars which the corporation contributes to the Trust rather than the after-tax dollars which would have been employed had the corporation tendered directly.

> Tendering for the stock through the ESOT gives the buyer a fifty-four precent edge over the after-tax purchase route. If the ESOT offers a higher price than the corporation would have been able to offer, it is more likely to be successful in its tender.

What happens when the ESOT has caused the corporation to *go private?* The stock price no longer varies in accordance with public reaction. It is determined by independent third party appraisal. The ESOT stands ready to buy stock from the founders or other remaining stockholders as they may wish to dispose of shares. It is not necessary that they sell out completely. The stock will perform in accordance with the actual performance of the company, rather than according to what the public thinks the company may be worth.

How The ESOT Can Strengthen The Market Or Stock Of A Public Company

Supply and demand determine the price of stock of public companies. If the ESOT buys a company's stock on the open market this should have a salutary effect on maintaining the price level of the stock.

> The ESOT serves as just another stockholder—but it can become one of significance.

The covered employees eventually receive distributions of their vested increments of the Trust in the form of shares of the stock. This should also eventually create a wider market for the stock. Those employees who own stock might tend to purchase more, thus enhancing the demand for the stock.

> The Department of Corporations of various states may reserve the prerogative of approving issuance of new stock. This or any other state requirement should be reviewed by counsel.

23.

How Banks Can Increase Their Lending Capacity Through An ESOT

Banks' earnings are, to a great measure, a direct reflection of their lending capability. A favorite rule of thumb has put the ratio at about five dollars of loans that can be generated for each dollar in reserves. The complications of modern-day banking has modified this ratio to some slight degree but it is still a truism that banks can leverage money into vastly greater quantities of loans —ergo, greater profits.

> Assuming no offsetting cash disbursement, one dollar of increased cash flow can be the resultant of one dollar of top savings, which in turn, can come about through the implementation of an ESOT.

> A bank can increase its lending capability through the following uses of an ESOT:

> 1. The bank can contribute newly-issued stock to the Trust. The

resultant tax savings increase the bank's cash flow and working capital, enabling it to expand its lending capacity.

2. A bank, with IRS approval, converts its profit-sharing plan to an ESOT, which then liquidates the assets, using the proceeds to buy shares of the bank's stock thus increasing net worth and lending capacity.

The ancillary effects for the bank can be substantial. The ESOT's shares become a focal point for the bank employees' retirement. It should encourage profit-orientation in their daily activities.

The ESOT may indeed become a major stockholder. Since the board of directors controls the vote of the ESOT, this provides a great mechanism for control of the stock and avoidance of a takeover in the case of a public company.

How a Bank's Trust Department Can Become More Profitable Through ESOT's

As executor and Trustee of many estates, a bank finds itself in many "can-of-worm" situations that cause Trust officers sleepless nights. It is not uncommon to find estates that control a majority block of closely-held stock or thinly-held public stock with no way of cashing out at other than a distressed price. There is no market for the non-public stock. Offering a large block of thinly-held public stock would tend to depress the price. The bank could be criticized if it holds onto a stagnant stock and subject to litigation if it sells at what might be considered to be a ridiculously low price. Damned if it does and damned if it doesn't.

If the corporation has a decent track record and is paying taxes in the top bracket, an ESOT might be just what the doctor ordered. Here is how the "bail out" works:

The corporation installs an ESOT to which it contributes deductible cash in amounts not to exceed 15% of covered payroll. The ESOT purchases stock from the executor of the estate at a price determined by third party appraisal, thereby avoiding criticism. This provides liquidity with which the executor can pay taxes or diversify the holdings in the estate. A loan might have come into play if needed. The Banks Trust department breathes a sigh of relief. In upholding its fiduciary role, it no longer needs to cast a wary eye to see that the business is still afloat. Without such a mechanism as ESOT, the business might be subject to liquidation to pay the estate taxes. The corporation maintains its executive staff which might have drifted away because of the uncertain future of the stock's control. Chances are, the bank will retain a corporate customer that may otherwise have been lost.

If the corporation had a profit-sharing plan, a game plan could have called for converting it to an ESOT and, with IRS approval, transferring the assets from the profit-sharing plan to the ESOT which liquidates the assets for the purchase of stock from the estate. Additional cash contributions could also be used to buy stock.

Insurance could be purchased by the ESOT on the life of the corporation's key executive to assure replacement of lost profits if he dies and payment of indebtedness to the estate if a note was involved in the acquisition of the stock. Forty-six cent dollars would be used to buy both the stock and the insurance due to the deductibility of the corporate contributions.

The Bank's Role In Preserving The Closely-Held Company

Where a bank serves as Trustee on behalf of a grantor of a Trust who is a major stockholder of a closely-held corporation, it would be wise to urge the corporation to consider implementing an ESOT. The primary purpose of the ESOT would be to purchase the large block of stock upon the stockholder's death. The ESOT would enter a Buy-Sell Agreement with the stockholder so that upon his death the ESOT could buy and his executor would sell at the price prevailing at the time of death as determined by independent appraisal.

24.

How To Increase The Capital Base Of A Savings And Loan Association With An Esot

A savings and loan association and a bank have much in common. Their capital base is a prime determinant of their profitability. They both make money by lending it. When a depositor leaves money with a bank, the institution earns a greater amount of this sum than it pays to the depositor. Both houses of finance have the ability to leverage the deposits.

An ESOT can improve the savings and loan association's lending capability in the same way as it can for a bank. The capital base is increased by the tax savings generated by a contribution of newly-issued stock. The cash flow increase is due to the fact that no cash outlay is required to obtain a tax deduction.

Both banks and savings and loan associations can increase their capital base through the acquisition route. Bank or savings and loan branches can be acquired through the ESOT by the use of pre-tax contributions that were placed into the ESOT by the corporation.

25.

Why Stockbrokers Tell Their Prospects Or Clients About The ESOT

If a stockbroker's prospective client happens to be a major shareholder in a private or a public company he may be unable to take advantage of viable investment opportunities because most of his assets are tied to his company's stock and he is suffering from a dearth of liquidity.

> The major stockholder in a private company has no market for his stock. The major stockholder in a public company has to wait for the secondary offering to clear.

The implementation of an Employee Stock Ownership Trust could make cash readily available for buying a sufficient number of his shares to enable him to start diversifying the shareholder's investment portfolio.

> The corporation itself might become a client as a result of the increased working capital and cash flow brought about by the ESOT.

The stockbroker might suggest that the company acquire some good dividend-paying preferred stock. The corporation receives favorable tax treatment, since 85% of the dividend is received by the company tax-free. The corporation is only subject to a tax on 15% of the dividend.

The increased cash flow resulting from the ESOT could be invested in the corporation's pension or profit-sharing plan, thereby creating more cash for the Trustees of those programs to invest through the stockholder.

The very act of bringing an exciting corporation-building idea to the president's attention is sufficient reason in itself to create a client relationship between the stockbroker and the shareholder.

Those stockbrokers who sell life insurance can sell blocks of insurance whose face amount equals the value of the corporation. The purpose of the insurance would be the funding of an ESOT/Shareholder Buy-Sell Agreement.

26.

How Investment Bankers And Venture Capital Specialists Can Increase Their Effectiveness Through ESOT's

ESOT's can prove their worth dramatically during periods of short money supply and high interest rates. It is at such times that investment bankers and venture capital specialists experience their most difficult challenges.

The ability of ESOT's to help a corporation increase its working capital, net worth and cash flow has been demonstrated. Any enhancement of these bookkeeping measurements represents an improvement in the company's fiscal well being. The healthier the corporation, the easier it is to attract capital.

A company whose ESOT has enabled it to improve its cash flow and working capital will not rely as much on outside suppliers of capital. The better its cash flow, the easier the debt servicing and the more attractive the potential borrower appears to a bank.

The leveraging capabilities, whereby the ESOT borrows cash which it repays with pre-tax company contributions, can be useful to a venture capital specialist. This characteristic reduces the lender's vulnerability to loss, thereby making him more responsive to the borrower's call. It permits repayment of the loan in about half the time it would have taken without the ESOT.

It would be well for such financial marriage counselors to consider advising their clients to explore the feasability of an Employee Stock Ownership Trust before attempting to finalize the financing. It might make the job easier.

27.

How Life Or Casualty Insurance Agencies And Companies Can Grow With ESOT's

The natural forces of competition coupled with the battering assaults of consumerism, compounded by unsympathetic legislation, have served to narrow the insurance companies' profit margins considerably.

If a life or casualty insurance company is to keep profits at their highest level, management must continue to be imaginative and receptive to new ideas.

> Premium income is the ultimate source of revenue. Profits result from favorable investment, claim and expense experience.

Insurors can write business through independent agencies, through company agencies, or on a direct basis, such as through direct mail or newspaper advertising, which bypasses the agent. The vast majority of companies rely upon agents in achieving sales goals. An insurance carrier wishing to expand through the agency route might consider incorporating each of its agencies which would, in turn, install an ESOT. The incorporated agency could contribute new stock to the Trust which would produce a greater cash flow, as we have determined in previous chapters.

> This additional cash flow can help the agency expand its facilities and its sales force, which ultimately benefits the insuror in the form of added business.

The ESOT can be the conduit through which bank loans are channeled to buy stock from the company. The corporation can find many uses for this new working capital, the repayment for which will have been made with pre-tax dollars. The corporation, of course, contributes cash to the ESOT amounting to 15% of covered payroll, and deducts this from taxable income.

> Each agency can acquire other agencies through the ESOT using pre-tax dollars, as we have seen earlier. The additional agencies add to the payroll base, thereby increasing the allowable corporate contribution to the tax-qualified Trust.

> A casualty insurance agency with which we are familiar did just that and within a few years had acquired other agencies and had quadrupled its payroll base and its permissable ESOT contribution. The leverage which the acquired agencies provided helped pay for themselves. The employees enjoy the satisfaction of having a beneficial interest in shares of the Trust that owns shares of the corporation which is the principal owner of the firms to which the employees are devoting their working years.

An insurance company could institute an ESOT for its own purposes on a direct basis with the insuror acquiring profitable agencies that have a substantial payroll base. The more the payroll increases, the greater the potential for enhancing cash flow or leveraging for expansion with pre-tax dollars.

28.

Practical Ways To Use Life Insurance In ESOT's—All With Pre-Tax Corporate Dollars

Life insurance on the life of an individual where the ESOT is the owner-beneficiary is treated as follows: Since the Employee Stock Ownership Trust is a tax-exempt Trust, there is no tax consequence if the premium is paid by the Trust or if the death proceeds are received by the Trust as beneficiary. The cash contributions made to the ESOT by the corporation are deductible by the corporation within the quantitative limits outlined earlier. In the final analysis, the insurance in the ESOT is acquired with dollars that had not previously been eroded by income taxes.

Here Are Some Creative Practical Ways To Use Life Insurance In ESOT's— All With Pre-Tax Corporate Dollars:

1. Fund Buy-Sell Agreement Between Stockholders And The ESOT. ESOT is owner-beneficiary and premium payor. Upon the stockholder's death, the ESOT buys his stock from his estate with the

death proceeds. Participants in the ESOT receive an interest in a greater number of shares of the company, thereby enhancing their security. The decedent's estate receives cash with which to meet its tax liabilities. The employees need not be concerned about the possibility of outside interests buying the decedent's stock from the estate and taking over.

> The amount of insurance should be equal to the value of the stock held by the key stockholders who are party to the agreement.

2. Keyman Insurance.

(a) On the Life of the Big Profit-Maker—

where the ESOT pays the premium and is owner-beneficiary of the policy. Tax treatment is the same as for funding a Buy-Sell Agreement. The life insurance offsets the potential reduction in stock valuation occasioned by the keyman's death.

> Loss of a sales manager can create substantial profit erosion. A $100,000 policy on his life, purchased by the ESOT, would be equal to an after-tax profit on two million dollars of sales, assuming five percent net after-tax profits.

(b) On the Lives of All Key Employees—

not just the few at the top. If any key employee dies, the dollars from the life insurance proceeds flow into the Trust to preserve the stock's value during the costly replacement period. Use of the Frisch Plan provides this coverage with no corporate after-tax cash outlay.

> The net equity in the Frisch Plan (the residual cash remaining in the policy owned by the ESOT even after the net corporate outlay zeros out) can be used to buy company stock.

This newly-created net equity cash from policies on the lives of a number of key employees can be used by the corporation to buy corporate-owned insurance in larger amounts on one or two of the key employees whose death might deal a crippling blow to the company's profitability.

Net Result:

Not only is the ESOT-owned insurance netted out at a zero corporate after-tax outlay, but the corporate owned keyman insurance is purchased with the previously non-existent increment of corporate cash flow eminating from the purchase of company stock by the use of the net-equity in the ESOT-keyman Frisch Plan.

The corporate-owned keyman insurance can be minimum deposited (cash value borrowed from the policy) and the cash value used as a cash contribution to the ESOT or pension plan. The corporation could, by paying four out of the first seven premiums, deduct the interest. The company can also deduct the borrowed cash value when it invests it in a tax-qualified Trust.

3. Use Of Earmarked Funds To Buy Insurance On Third Party's Life:

An ESOT can function as a profit-sharing plan in that the corporation can contribute cash to the Trust in lieu of stock. An employee-participant can authorize the administrative committee to direct the trustees to use some or all of his vested account in the ESOT to pay insurance premiums on his own life, or on the life of a third party such as a keyman or a major stockholder.

The Trust would be the beneficiary and the purpose might be to preserve the value of the participants' accounts in the event a keyman died. Or, in the case of a stockholder in a thinly-held public company, the proceeds would help replace the loss if the stockholder's executors were forced to dump the stock on the market. The insured might be the one whose vested account was earmarked to buy *the insurance.*

The ESOT participant whose account pays for the premium will benefit in the death proceeds to the extent that his participation bears to the total in the Trust. He may have a significant stake in the total assets of the Trust or he may simply be motivated by concern for his co-participants who may be his employees.

4. Use Of Previously Deducted Cash To Buy Tax-Deductible Insurance:

Deduction #1—

Section 79 of the IRC permits a corporation, under certain circumstances, to deduct premiums on the lives of selected categories of employees. The employees may name anyone beneficiary but the corporation. The employee pays no tax on the first $50,000 of face amount of the insurance. He incurs only a modest taxable income liability on the excess—much less than the premium (Table 1 tax rates are used—not P.S. 58 rates).

Deduction #2—

The *corporation makes a deductible cash contribution to its ESOT. The ESOT uses the cash to buy company stock, thus putting cash back into the corporation.* It is this previously-deducted cash that is used to buy the deductible insurance.

5. Use Of Previously-Deducted Cash To Fund Corporate-Owned Keyman Or Stock Redemption:

Depending upon whether the corporation chooses to contribute stock or cash to the ESOT, cash either remains in the corporation through increased cash flow occasioned by tax savings, or cash comes back to the company with ESOT purchases of corporate stock. In either event, the corporation can use the recovered cash to pay premiums for corporate-owned keyman insurance or insurance to fund a Buy-Sell Agreement between the corporation and the stockholders.

A variation of the Frisch Plan can be employed by having the corporation borrow the cash value increase from the policy each year. This borrowed cash can be used as part of the tax-deductible annual contribution to the ESOT. The ESOT can, thereupon, use this cash to buy company stock. The cycle is complete. It is repeated each year.

Summary:

The corporation deducts the original cash contribution to the ESOT.

The ESOT uses it to buy stock from the company.

The company uses the cash (which has already been deducted) to pay insurance premiums.

The corporation borrows the available cash value.

The corporation uses the borrowed cash value as an ESOT contribution.

An ESOT should be so worded that the Trustee is permitted to use Trust assets for the purchase of insurance. Unless this is the case, some of these insurance opportunities could not occur. These techniques should be implemented only under guidance of counsel.

29.

Disadvantages Of An ESOT

The ESOT is not a panacea. There are many specific things that a corporation can do for itself and for its stockholders that can be accomplished through alternate routes.

It is difficult, however, to envision any other single document that will provide a viable solution for such a variety of financial and strategic corporate problems while providing an important fringe benefit to employees.

Where advantages are so prevalent, there are bound to be disadvantages. The ESOT is no exception.

Dilution seems to be a key disadvantage. By issuing new stock so as to make a tax-deductible contribution to the Trust, the value of each share is reduced. The question is whether the advantages such as the increase in working capital and cash flow occasioned by the tax savings will offset the adverse effects of dilution.

It is also apparent that if the stock of the employer does poorly on a consistent basis the retirement values of the employees will suffer.

> Of course, if the corporation does not do well for a sufficiently long period it is likely that the employee may not survive in that capacity to retirement age. The business will probably go under and the employee's primary concern will be one of immediate pre-retirement security.

The infusion of working capital through the ESOT should enhance the value of the stock and the ultimate survival of the firm and the jobs.

> ESOT investments can be varied to the same extent as in a pension or a profit-sharing Trust. Thus, cash contributions to the ESOT can provide security through diversification if desired.

An employer can also adopt a pension plan in addition to the ESOT. The former can invest in traditional pension Trust investments while the latter can invest in the company's stock—either common or preferred. If preferred stock is contributed, dividends paid into the Trust will build up on a tax-deferred basis, thus providing a further measure of security.

> Another disadvantage, if it can be so categorized, is the fact that someday the corporation must exercise the participant's put with hard dollars, assuming the plan contains such a provision.

Unless the ESOP is monitored with forethought it is conceivable that a shift in control might occur. Sometimes this is the intent. There are safeguards which would tend to avoid a loss of control.

30.

The Social Significance Of ESOT

So-called fringe benefit programs have proliferated since World War II. Group life and medical benefits have become as much a part of the industrial scene as the punch-out clock.

> Pensions and profit-sharing plans have joined the take-it-for-granted rights of millions of employees. These benefits are important to the well-being of those who work for the captains of industry, but they are relatively superficial.

Profit-sharing plans, for example, are generally not a true reflection of the intrinsic profits of the corporation. Such plans do not distribute the capital growth which is enhanced by profits. A portion of the profits may be contributed to the Profit-Sharing Trust as the board of directors may direct. Not all the profits, and certainly none of the capital appreciation, is distributed to the Trust for the benefit of the employees who helped to create the growth.

A practical as well as an emotional barrier exists between those who own the company and those who work for the company. The former get the paycheck, a gold watch, and if they are born under the right star, a cash distribution related to the amount of cash the board chose to contribute to the Trust. This sum is generally quite unrelated to the capital growth the company experienced during the employee's tenure.

The ESOT forms a bond between those who build the company and those who own it. They eventually can become one and the same and all are the better for it. By contributing its own equity securities to the Trust, the corporation is receiving nourishment vis-a-vis the 54% tax saving. The company's management employs this portion of its profits toward achieving capital growth instead of using it to subsidize the government directly.

The participating employees of the ESOT share in this capital growth and thereby add to the ranks of the capitalists.

As their company grows, so do they. This mechanism strengthens corporations and creates employment. Working individuals pay taxes. Those who are unemployed take taxes. Containment of the pre-retirement welfare population is enhanced by the ESOT. The post-retirement dependency upon Social Security is minimized.

This, then, forms the basis of logic for the Employee Stock Ownership Plan.

31.

History Of ESOT

Employee Stock Ownership Plans and Trusts have been on the American scene since the 1930's. The Stock Bonus Plan was the forerunner of the Employee Stock Ownership Plan, a name that is generally attributed to Louis O. Kelso, an attorney and economist who long ago envisioned the many social advantages that could be derived from the ESOP.

> The Sears Plan is perhaps the best known ESOP in effect. Sears has contributed its own stock to its Trust since the Plan's inception. Many Sears employees have become wealthy retirees as a result of the growth of the company's securities in the Trust.

It has been estimated that as of the early 1970's, there were fewer than five hundred ESOT's in existence. Recognition of the virtues of the concept is expanding the number of firms that have adopted such plans.

> An ever-increasing number of corporations are implementing Employee Stock Ownership Trusts with the altruisic intent of transferring complete ownership of the company from the sole stockholder to the employees.

Now that the words "Employee Stock Ownership Plan" appear in the Employee Retirement Income Security Act of 1974 it is anticipated that an upsurge of plans will be effected.

The Tax Reduction Act of 1975 provides further evidence of governmental recognition of the social attributes of ESOT's. The intent of the Act was to stimulate the economy by increasing the investment credit from 7% to 10% for those who invest in certain categories of equipment and construction.

The new law increases the investment credit from 10% to 11% for corporations having or installing Employee Stock Ownership Trusts structured in accordance with certain guidelines. This provision of the law is effective from January 22, 1975 to December 31, 1976.

32.

Implementing The ESOT

The Employee Stock Ownership Trust is not for every company. The profile of likely candidates for ESOT provides an overview of firms that should explore an ESOT's possibilities. It is important to determine the basic goals of those who control the corporation being evaluated as an ESOT candidate.

> The strength, structure, and earning capacity of a company must be considered as well. The Employee Stock Ownership Feasibility Checklist on subsequent pages can be useful in uncovering these facts.

> A review of the Corp, Inc., Feasibility Study will demonstrate the effect of an ESOT on the corporate financials of this fictitious company. A study of this kind should be undertaken prior to arriving at a final decision to implement an ESOT.

Assuming the corporation's board of directors resolves to adopt an ESOT, a

Plan and Trust would be prepared by counsel for the board's review and submission to the local District Director of Internal Revenue for a Letter of Determination.

> It is desirable to use a corporate Trustee such as a bank. However, an individual could serve as Trustee. Generally, an administrative committee composed of interested parties is employed in addition to the Trustee. Annual administration is quite similar to that of a profit-sharing plan. There are qualified administrators who are well equipped to serve in that function.

> It is important that those in a fiduciary capacity keep the provisions of the 1974 Pension Reform Legislation in mind in the implementation and maintenance of an ESOT.

> The periodic reports show the number of shares in the total account and in each participant's account, the value of the shares held in the Trust, the value of each participant's account, and the value of his vested interest.

Annual tax forms similar to those required for other qualified plans must be submitted to IRS. Some states require the completion of additional reporting forms.

Summary Of Steps To Implement ESOT:

1. Feasibility study
2. Evaluation of the corporate stock
3. Design of plan
4. Resolution by board of directors to adopt ESOT (Plan and Trust) drafted by counsel
5. Contribution by corporation during tax year
6. Communication of plan to employees
7. Submission to IRS for Letter of Determination
8. Administration of plan

33.

Profile Of Likely Candidates For ESOT

Corporation in top income tax bracket with likelihood of remaining profitable.

Corporation taxed as a corporation—not a Sub-Chapter S Corporation.
    (Sub-Chapter S Corporations do not qualify.)

Must be a domestic corporation.

Corporations may be privately or publicly owned.

Professional corporations would not qualify unless a method were found to avoid distribution of shares to non-professionals, including heirs. A number of states will not permit a trust to own shares of a professional corporation.
    (e.g., Only doctors can own shares of a medical professional corporation.)

Corporation desiring to make acquisitions.
(Corporation can do this with pre-tax dollars.)

Corporation desiring to make divestiture.
(Corporation can facilitate this by making it possible for buyers to take over with pre-tax dollars.)

Private corporation whose major or minor stockholders wish to cash out.
(The ESOT provides a private pre-tax method for accomplishing this.)

Public corporation wishing to avoid takeover.
(ESOT can tender for shares. Present management would appoint the committee that directs the voting of the Trust.)

Corporation whose major stockholders desire creative and tax advantageous methods in their estate planning.

Corporations that have incurred debt of anticipated future financing.
(Principal and interest can be serviced with pre-tax dollars through the ESOT. $500,000 of principal can be serviced with $500,000 by using the pre-tax dollar approach through the ESOT. Without this method a corporation would be required to earn $1.25 million to repay a $500,000 loan.)

Corporations that have profit-sharing plans.
(It may be possible to convert to an ESOT, thereby using the assets to buy company stock.)

34.

Employee Stock Ownership Trust Feasibility Checklist

Name of Corporation..
Address...
....
Date of Incorporation ....Fiscal Year Ends ....
Public?   Yes........ No........   If Yes, What Exchange...............................
Six Largest Stockholders:

| | No. of | | No. of |
| Stockholder | Shares | Stockholder | Shares |

1) ....   4) ....
2) ....   5) ....
3) ....   6) ....

Corporation's Estimated Worth: $........................

	No. of Employees	Payroll
Non-Union	....	$....................
Union	....	$....................

(Attach detailed breakdown of employee data by subsidiary.)

125

Financial Summary for Preceding Three Years:

	Taxable Income	Taxes Paid
19........	$....................	$....................
19........	$....................	$....................
19........	$....................	$....................

Estimated Taxable Income for Current Year: $.................... .
(Attach financial statements for past three years.)

Projection for Next Three Years:

	Sales	Net Income
19........	$....................	$....................
19........	$....................	$....................
19........	$....................	$....................

Corporate Capitalization:

	Common Stock	Preferred Stock
Authorized	....	....
Outstanding	....	....

Long Term Debt:

Maturity	Interest	Amount
....	....	....
....	....	....
....	....	....

What Are The Objectives In Considering ESOT?

Check:

..........Finance Debit   ....Raise Capital
..........Motivate Employees   ....Convert Profit-Sharing Plan
..........Create Market For Stock ....Other..........................
..........Increase Cash Flow

(Attach copies of profit-sharing or pension plans, covered employee data, asset value and annual contribution history since adoption.)

35.

Corp, Inc., Feasibility Study

Table of Contents

EXHIBIT I
  A Case Study—Corp, Inc., Profile

EXHIBIT II
  Five Year Estimated Projection:
  Pre-Tax Income, ESOT Participants' Payroll and Corporate Contributions to the ESOT

EXHIBIT III
  Five Year Cash Flow Projection. Assumption: No ESOT

EXHIBIT IV
  Five Year Cash Flow Projection. Assumption: ESOT All Contributions In Stock

EXHIBIT V
    Five Year Cash Flow Projection:
    No Loan Involved
    Assumption: Corporate Contribution Of Cash And Stock To ESOT

EXHIBIT VI
    Five Year Cash Flow Projection:
    Loan Involved. No ESOT

EXHIBIT VII
    Five Year Cash Flow Projection:
    Loan Involved
    Assumption: Corporate Contributions Of Cash And Stock To ESOT

SUMMARY
    Corp, Inc., Feasibility Study

EXHIBIT I
A CASE STUDY
CORP, INC., PROFILE

Date Of Incorporation:	July 1, 1960
Fiscal Year End:	December 31
Nature Of Activity:	Manufacturer of small electric motors
Growth Pattern:	Average 10% annual increase in pre-tax net income last six years
Number Of Employees:	Total number: 210
	ESOT participants: 170
	Union employees: none
ESOT Payroll:	$1,800,000
Existing Pension Or Profit-Sharing Plans:	None
Current Year's Taxable Income:	$190,000
Public Or Private Ownership:	Private
If Private, Names Of Stockholders And % Owned:	
	Mr. R. Corp........80%
	Mrs. J. Proc........20%

EXHIBIT II
CORP, INC.
FIVE YEAR ESTIMATED PROJECTION
PRE-TAX INCOME, ESOT PARTICIPANTS' PAYROLL
AND CORPORATE CONTRIBUTIONS TO THE ESOT

1. Fiscal Years Ending Dec. 31	2. Pre-Tax Income	3. ESOT Participants' Payroll	4. Corporate Contribution To ESOT
1975	$ 190,000	$ 1,800,000	$ 255,000
1976	200,000	1,900,000	200,000
1977	210,000	2,000,000	210,000
1978	220,000	2,100,000	220,000
1979	230,000	2,200,000	230,000
TOTALS	$1,050,000	$10,000,000	$1,115,000

EXHIBIT III
CORP, INC.
FIVE YEAR CASH FLOW PROJECTION. ASSUMPTION: NO ESOT

Fiscal Yr. Ending Dec. 31	1975	1976	1977	1978	1979
Pre-Tax Income	$190,000	$200,000	$210,000	$220,000	$230,000
Fed. & State Income Tax (A)	95,190	100,200	105,210	110,220	115,230
Cash Flow And Net Income	94,810	99,800	104,790	109,780	114,770

Aggregate Five Year Cash Flow: $523,950

(A) Combined Federal and State effective income tax rate assumed to be 50.1% for purpose of these calculations. (54% top bracket averaged with 25% lower bracket computed at $190,000 income level but used for convenience at all levels, not applicable in all states.)

Corp, Inc., Feasibility Study

EXHIBIT IV
CORP, INC.
FIVE YEAR CASH FLOW PROJECTION. ASSUMPTION: ESOT ALL CONTRIBUTIONS IN STOCK

Fiscal Yr. Ending Dec. 31	1975	1976	1977	1978	1979
1. Pre-Tax Income	$190,000	$200,000	$210,000	$220,000	$230,000
2. Minus Stock Contributions To ESOT	255,000	200,000	210,000	220,000	230,000
3. Taxable Income	(65,000)	-0-	-0-	-0-	-0-
4. Income Tax	(32,565)	-0-	-0-	-0-	-0-
5. Net After-Tax Income	(32,435)	-0-	-0-	-0-	-0-
6. Cash Flow (A)	222,565	200,000	210,000	220,000	230,000

Aggregate Five Year Cash Flow: $1,082,565

(A) Cash Flow = (1) minus (4)

EXHIBIT V
CORP, INC.
FIVE YEAR CASH FLOW PROJECTION
NO LOAN INVOLVED
ASSUMPTION: CORPORATE CONTRIBUTION OF CASH AND STOCK TO ESOT

Fiscal Yr. Ending Dec. 31	1975	1976	1977	1978	1979
1. Pre-Tax Income	$190,000	$200,000	$210,000	$220,000	$230,000
2. Minus Contributions To ESOT					
(a) Stock	127,245	99,800	104,790	109,780	115,770
(b) Cash	127,755	100,200	105,210	110,220	114,230
TOTAL	255,000	200,000	210,000	220,000	230,000
3. Taxable Income	(65,000)	-0-	-0-	-0-	-0-
4. Income Tax	(32,565)	-0-	-0-	-0-	-0-
5. Cash Flow (A)	94,810	99,800	104,790	109,780	115,770

Aggregate Five Year Cash Flow: $524,950

(A) Cash Flow = (1) minus (2)(B) minus (4)

EXHIBIT VI
CORP, INC.
FIVE YEAR CASH FLOW PROJECTION
LOAN INVOLVED. NO ESOT

Fiscal Yr. Ending Dec. 31	1975	1976	1977	1978	1979
1. Pre-Tax Income	$190,000	$200,000	$210,000	$220,000	$230,000
2. Minus Interest On Loan	15,000	12,000	9,000	6,000	3,000
3. Adjusted Taxable Income	175,000	188,000	201,000	214,000	227,000
4. Income Tax	87,675	94,188	100,701	107,214	113,727
5. Payment Toward (A) Principal	30,000	30,000	30,000	30,000	30,000
6. Cash Flow (B)	57,325	63,812	70,299	76,786	83,273

(A) Corporation borrows $150,000 at 10%. Principal being amortized in five equal annual installments.

(B) Cash Flow = (1) minus (2) minus (4) minus (5)

Aggregate Five Year Cash Flow: $351,495

EXHIBIT VII
CORP, INC.
FIVE YEAR CASH FLOW PROJECTION
LOAN INVOLVED
ASSUMPTION: CORPORATE CONTRIBUTIONS OF CASH AND STOCK TO ESOT

Fiscal Yr. Ending Dec. 31	1975	1976	1977	1978	1979
1. Pre-Tax Income	$190,000	$200,000	$210,000	$220,000	$230,000
2. Minus Contributions To ESOT					
(a) Stock	127,245	99,800	104,790	109,780	115,770
(b) Cash Or Note	45,000	42,000	66,210	36,000	33,000
(c) Cash for Liquidity	82,755	58,200	39,000	74,220	81,230
TOTAL	255,000	200,000	210,000	220,000	230,000
3. Taxable Income	(65,000)	-0-	-0-	-0-	-0-
4. Income Tax	(32,565)	-0-	-0-	-0-	-0-
5. Cash Flow (A)	94,810	99,800	104,790	109,780	115,770

Aggregate Five Year Cash Flow: $524,950

(A) Cash Flow = (1) minus (2)(B) minus (2)(C) minus 4

CORP, INC., FEASIBILITY STUDY
SUMMARY

EXHIBIT III:

No ESOT—(no loan involved)

Five-year cash flow—$523,950

EXHIBIT IV:

ESOT—(no loan involved)

All corporate contributions to the ESOT are in the form of the corporation's own stock.

Five-year cash flow (with ESOT).......... $1,082,565

Five-year cash flow (no ESOT) .... $ 523,950

Difference .... $ 558,615

Observations: The corporate contributions to an ESOT have maximized cash flow, improving it by $558,615 over the five-year period as compared with the cash flow where no ESOT exists.

In addition, the employees enjoy a valuable fringe benefit.

EXHIBIT V:

ESOT—(no loan involved)

Unlike the preceding exhibit, the corporate contribution consists of a combination of its own stock as well as cash.

Five-year cash flow (cash and stock contributions) to an ESOT—
....$524,950

Five-year cash flow (no ESOT)........$523,950

Although the cash flow is not as great as in the preceding exhibit, the cash flow is almost the same wherein there is no ESOT. But, in addition, the ESOT provides a valuable fringe benefit to the employees.

Cash contributions amounting to $557,615 over the five-year period can be used for purposes including but not limited to:

(a) Buying stock from stockholders—creating a market.
(b) Purchasing insurance on the lives of stockholders to fund a Buy-Sell Agreement.
(c) Retire debt.

EXHIBIT VI:

No ESOT—(loan involved)

This exhibit illustrates the effect of a $150,000 loan at 10% made directly to the corporation where no ESOT exists.

Five-year cash flow $351,495

EXHIBIT VII:

ESOT—(loan involved)

The aforementioned loan is made to and amortized by an ESOT. The corporation has made cash and stock contributions indicated in categories as follows:

(a) Stock
(b) Cash for note retirement
(c) Cash for liquidity

The amount of stock contributed is designed to produce the same cash flow as that which is produced in the exhibit wherein no ESOT or loan is involved.

The cash for liquidity can be used to purchase:

(a) Stock from stockholders—creating a market.
(b) Purchase insurance to fund a Buy-Sell Agreement between the stockholder and the ESOT.

Five-year cash flow $524,950

Observations: In addition to amortizing principal and interest, this exhibit demonstrates that cash can be provided to create a market for stockholders and provide for the estate planning liquidity needs with no change in cash flow. In addition to these obvious effects is the creation of a fine fringe benefit for employees.

RECOMMENDATION:

The implementation of an Employee Stock Ownership Plan is a viable concept for Corp, Inc.

Cash Flow:

The exhibits demonstrate that cash flow can be improved while providing the employees with a valuable fringe benefit. Fringe benefit stock valued at 15% of covered payroll can be contributed to the ESOT and apportioned in the Trust for the benefit of the employees in accordance with a formula related to their compensation.

The value of the stock at the time it is contributed, over the five year period, amounts to $1,115,000. This does not take into consideration any growth the stock might experience.

Tax Refund:

The corporation is eligible to receive a $40,080 tax refund by virtue of a 1975 contribution to the ESOT which can amount to $270,000, exceeding the $190,000 pre-tax income by $80,000, thus putting the company in a loss position by that amount.

Liquid Asset and Cash Fund:

The illustration demonstrates that cash can be contributed in combination with stock, the sum in this instance amounting to $557,615. The cash can be used to:

(a) Purchase insurance to fund a Buy-Sell Agreement between shareholders and the ESOT.
(b) Purchase stock directly from the shareholders.
(c) Make an acquisition.

Corporate Planning Flexibility:

> The corporation can adjust its taxable income and its cash flow.
> It can "cash-out" minority stockholders.
> The company can refinance indebtedness.
> It can make acquisitions with pre-tax dollars.

Debt Reduction:

> Servicing debt, using pre-tax dollars to liquidate principal and interest is feasible as indicated in the exhibits.

> New financing can be contemplated more readily where an ESOT exists.

It is therefore recommended that Corp, Inc., implement an ESOT prior to the end of the fiscal year.

36.

How Some Corporations May Be Able To Get Preferential Consideration For A Low Interest Government-Backed Loan Through ESOT's

The Trade Act of 1974 provides for a $500,000,000 U.S. Government fund for backing loans to businesses in "trade impacted areas," that is, in communities which might be adversely affected by imports from abroad.

> Corporations, or subdivisions of corporations, for example, that manufacture textiles, electronic components, shoes or widgets, may be eligible for such loans if competition from abroad threatens to result in a decline in sales or possible layoffs of workers.

Of particular interest is the specific mention of Employee Stock Ownership Trusts in the Act. Section 273(f)(1) of the Act says that preference shall be given to a corporation which agrees that 25% of the principal amount of the loan is paid by the lender to an Employee Stock Ownership Trust "maintained by the recipient corporation, by a parent or subsidiary of such corporation, or by several corporations including the recipient corporations..."

The Act further states that the amount of the loan to the qualified Trust will be used to purchase qualified employer securities, and that the ESOT will service principal and interest out of amounts contributed to the Trust by the recipient corporation.

The Section stipulates that from time to time, as the qualified Trust repays the loan, the Trust "shall allocate to the accounts of participating employees that portion of the qualified securities the cost of which bears substantially the same ratio to the cost of all employer securities purchased under... this subsection as the amount of the loan principal and interest repaid by the qualified Trust during that year bears to the total amount of the loan principal and interest payable by such Trust during the term of such loan."

The allocation of securities allocated to each participant is in the same proportion that his compensation bears to all participants during that year.

The U.S. Government in providing this opportunity gives further sanction to ESOT's.

In effect, the Trade Act of 1974 permits not only preferential treatment to those companies that install an ESOT, but it actually allows the loan to the ESOT to be serviced with pre-tax dollars. The government is, therefore, paying part of the principal and interest on the loan which it backs.

The securities must be common voting stock which is voted by the participants when it is allocated.

The Act must be studied in its entirety and acted upon only upon advice of counsel.

37.

Questions And Answers

Q. Can the following answers or other comments in this book always be relied upon as accurate or unchangeable?
A. Unfortunately—or fortunately—regulations and their interpretations change from time to time. A multitude of regulatory authorities may interject their influence. One's authority should be his legal counsel. The contents of this book should not be considered a final authority, but should be used only to stimulate one's thinking on the subject of ESOT's for further investigation.

Q. Who participates in the ESOT?
A. Employees who meet stipulated eligibility requirements. Shares of the Trust assets are apportioned according to a formula.

Q. Are distributions made in stock or cash?
A. Stock.

Q. When?

A. Upon termination of employment an employee is entitled to his vested interest. The Trust may authorize the employee's account to remain in the Trust until normal retirement age if done on a non-discriminatory basis.

Q. Do employees become stockholders while participating in an ESOT?

A. No. The Trust owns the stock. Employees have no direct rights as stockholders unless they own stock aside from that in the Trust.

Q. When employee-participants get stock, say at retirement, what do they do with it?

A. The Trust can be worded in a variety of ways. For example, the employee could be given a put to sell the stock at its then current valuation to the corporation or to other stockholders. Some ESOT's have been designed to have the Trust buy the terminated employee's stock.

Q. What is a primary negative of an ESOT?

A. Dilution of the stock. Hopefully, the adverse effect of dilution will be more than offset by the beneficial results of increased cash flow and working capital made possible by the ESOT.

Q. How is the value of the stock of a closely-held company determined?

A. There are firms that specialize in valuing stock. Factors such as earnings, net worth, price of similar public companies' stock, and stability of company are considered.

Q. Can the ESOT be combined with a money purchase pension plan under a single document?

A. Apparently. The two plans can be laminated. An ESOP is an eligible individual account plan defined as "a stock bonus plan which is qualified or a stock bonus plan and money purchase pension plan, both of which are qualified under Section 401 of the Internal Revenue Code of 1954, and which is designed to invest primarily in qualifying employer securities . . ."
A money purchase plan, or a stock bonus plan, unless they are eligible individual account plans cannot invest more than 10% of their assets in employer securities. In the broad ESOP definition, however, the two plans

can be designed as a combination which would permit a corporation to contribute up to 25% of eligible payroll, including forfeitures, all in company stock.

Q. *Does this mean that a stock bonus plan or a money purchase pension plan is an ESOP?*
A. No. In order that they be permitted to acquire more employer stock than the 10% rule permits, the plans must be eligible individual account plans. The ESOP must make distributions in employer stock.

Q. *Must those in a fiduciary capacity be bonded?*
A. Yes. By a fidelity bond.

Q. *Accelerated funding is a requirement for inadequately funded mixed benefit pension plans. Is this applicable to ESOP's?*
A. No.

Q. *Plan termination insurance is a prerequisite in fixed benefit pension plans. How about in ESOP's?*
A. Not required.

Q. *Tax qualified trusts for employees requires a fair return on the investment. Does an ESOT, by investing in employer stock, violate this rule?*
A. No. This requirement is waived for ESOP's.

Q. *May existing life insurance policies be transferred to an ESOT?*
A. Some could possibly pose a transfer for value problem. Also, it is a transaction that might violate the rules relating to parties in interest. Cases should be considered on the basis of circumstances as well as current or future rulings.

Q. *Can 100% of ESOT funds be invested in company stock?*
A. Yes.

Q. *Should employees be permitted to make contributions to an ESOT?*
A. Preferably not, particularly in a private company, since the stock might have to be registered with the SEC.

Q. Can the ESOT funds be invested in prudent investments other than company stock?

A. Yes.

Q. What forms of company stock can be purchased by the ESOT?

A. Common or preferred, voting or non-voting, cumulative or non-cumulative, convertible preferred or any other kind that is considered eligible securities under the law.

Q. Debt security?

A. Not unless the debt security meets the 1974 Reform Act's definition of a "marketable security."

Q. Should a public company obtain a no-action letter from the SEC or investigate other SEC requirements before it attempts to go private?

A. By all means.

Q. May dividends be passed through to participants?

A. Yes.

Q. Does an ESOT require an annual actuarial evaluation?

A. No. A fixed benefit pension plan does, but an ESOT does not.

38.

Sample Of An Employee Stock Ownership Plan

The following Plan is based on hypothetical facts of a fictional company. It is not a "Model" Plan. It is designed to meet most, but not necessarily all of the requirements arising under ERISA. Therefore, this Plan must be examined in relation to ERISA and to the regulations under ERISA when they are issued. Such regulations may require drastic changes in many provisions set forth and the addition or deletion of other provisions. This Plan should be treated with caution by counsel as being merely a series of suggestions to them and should not be used except by attorneys who can modify this Plan to meet all of the ERISA requirements to fit the needs of their clients and who become reasonably competent in the specific requirements of ERISA and qualified plans in general.

Marvin Goodson, Esq.
Marvin Goodson Professional Corp.
Los Angeles, California

Marvin Goodson is an attorney and is a principal of Marvin Goodson Professional Corporation. He has lectured extensively on tax matters for tax institutes, tax forums, educational programs, and similar organizations. He is the author of various articles on taxation. He is a member of the American Bar Association Section on Taxation and the American Institute of Certified Public Accountants. Mr. Goodson was active in Washington to help communicate a fuller understanding of the many uses, benefits, and problems of ESOTS from the point of view of the practicing ESOT lawyer to many of the authors of ERISA and their staffs. This Plan was drawn by Marvin Goodson as part of an article on ESOTS appearing in the Executive Compensation Journal. It is reprinted with the permission of Tax Management, Inc.

JONES MANUFACTURING, INC.

EMPLOYEE STOCK OWNERSHIP PLAN

Section I. **Nature of Plan.**

    A. The purpose of this Plan is to enable participating employees of the Company to share in the growth and prosperity of the Company and to provide participants with an opportunity to accumulate capital for their future economic security. The Plan is designed to do this without any deductions from participants' paychecks or without calling upon them to invest their personal savings. A primary purpose of the Plan is to enable participants to acquire a proprietary interest in the Company. Consequently, the Company contributions made to the Trust will be invested primarily in Company stock.

    B. This Plan, effective as of January 1, 1975, is intended to qualify as a stock bonus plan under section 401(a) of the Internal Revenue Code ("Code") and which is defined in section 4975 (e)(7) of the Code and in section 407(d)(6) of the Employee Retirement Income Security Act of 1974 (the "Act") and consists of the Plan and the Trust Agreement. All assets acquired under this Plan as a result of Company contributions, income and other additions to the Trust will be administered, distributed, forfeited and otherwise governed by the provisions of this Plan which is administered by the Committee for the exclusive benefit of participants in the Plan and their beneficiaries.

Section II. **Definitions.**

    In this Plan, whenever the context so indicates, the singular or plural number and the masculine, feminine or neuter gender shall each be deemed to include the other, the terms "he," "his," and "him" shall refer to a participant of either gender and the following words shall have the following meanings:

        ACCOUNT - The term "account" shall mean one of several accounts maintained to record the interest of a participant in the Plan.

APPROVED ABSENCE - The term "approved absence" shall mean an absence from work not exceeding one year, including absence due to temporary disability, granted to and approved for an employee by Company in a uniform and non-discriminatory manner; or an absence from work for service in the Armed Forces or other government services, provided that, and only so long as, reemployment rights are protected by law; or any layoff by Company, because of lack of work, not in excess of one year.

ANNIVERSARY DATE - The term "anniversary date" shall mean the 31st day of December of each year.

BENEFICIARY - The term "beneficiary" shall mean the person or persons entitled to receive any benefits under the Plan in the event of a participant's death.

BREAK-IN-SERVICE - The term "break-in-service" shall mean a calendar year beginning with a participant's first calendar year after becoming a participant in which a participant has completed 500 or less hours of service.

COMMITTEE - The Committee appointed by the Board of Directors of the Company to administer the Plan and to give instructions to the Trustee.

COMPANY - Jones Manufacturing, Inc., a California corporation.

COMPANY STOCK - The term "Company stock" shall mean shares of any class of stock, preferred or common, voting or non-voting, which are issued by the Company.

COMPANY STOCK ACCOUNT - The term "Company stock account" shall mean the account of a participant which is credited with the shares of Company stock purchased and paid for by the Trust or contributed to the Trust.

COVERED COMPENSATION - The term "covered compensation" shall mean the total gross compensation payable to a participant by the Company for each year before deductions required by law or agreement, including overtime compensation, and bonuses, but excluding deferred compensation and contributions to this or any other deferred compensation plan.

CURRENT OBLIGATIONS - The term "current obligations" shall mean Trust obligations arising from extension of credit to the Trust and payable in cash within one year from the date a Company contribution is due.

EMPLOYEE - The term "employee" shall mean any employee of Company.

EMPLOYER - The term "employer" shall mean Jones Manufacturing, Inc., a California corporation.

FORFEITURE - The term "forfeiture" shall mean the portion of a participant's accounts which does not become part of his plan benefit.

GENERAL OBLIGATIONS - The term "general obligations" shall mean Trust obligations not arising from extensions of credit to the Trust but which are commitments which arise from the Trust's authorized activities.

NON-CURRENT OBLIGATIONS - The term "non-current obligations" shall mean Trust obligations arising from extension of credit to the Trust and payable in cash more than one year from the date an employer contribution is due.

NORMAL RETIREMENT DATE - An employee's 65th birthday.

OTHER INVESTMENTS ACCOUNT - The term "other investments account" shall mean the account of a participant which is credited with his share of the net income (or loss) of the Trust and Company contributions and forfeitures in other than Company stock and which is debited with payments made to pay for Company stock.

PARTICIPANT - The term "participant" shall mean any employee who is participating in this Plan.

PARTICIPATING SERVICE - The term "participating service" is meant to include all years of service completed by an employee after he becomes a participant.

PLAN - The Jones Manufacturing, Inc. Employee Stock Ownership Plan, which includes this Plan and Trust Agreement, but does not include a Money Purchase Pension Plan if one is established by the Company or any other deferred compensation plan of Company.

PLAN YEAR - A calendar year.

PLAN BENEFIT - The term "plan benefit" shall mean the distribution to which a participant or his beneficiary becomes entitled upon termination of participation.

SEMI-ANNUAL ENTRY DATE - A January 1st and a July 1st after January 1, 1975.

SERVICE - The term "service" shall mean regular employment as an employee of Company.

TRUST - The Trust created by the Trust Agreement entered into between the Company and the Trustee.

TRUST AGREEMENT - The Agreement between the Company and the Trustee or any successor Trustee establishing the Trust and specifying the duties of the Trustee.

TRUSTEE - The Trustee (or Trustees) designated by the Company's Board of Directors (and any successor Trustee), which agrees to act by executing the Trust Agreement.

VESTED SERVICE - The term "vested service" shall mean all years of service (including years of service with Company and its predecessor Jones Partnership prior to the Act as if the Act had been in effect) subsequent to the plan year in which an employee attains age 22; service prior to a break-in-service is not included in vested service until the participant has completed a year of service after the break-in-service.

YEAR OF SERVICE - A 12 month period beginning with the participant's semi-annual entry date during which the employee has completed not less than 1,000 hours of service with the Company.

Section III. <u>Eligibility</u>.

All employees of Company as of January 1, 1975 who completed at least 1,000 hours of service in the calendar year 1974, shall be eligible to participate in this Plan as of the effective date. Every other employee will become a participant in this Plan on the semi-annual entry date next following his attainment of age 25 and the earlier of (a) the 12 month period following his employment by employer if he completes 1,000 hours of service during the period, or (b) the first plan year in which he completes 1,000 hours of service.

Section IV. <u>Participation</u>.

As of each anniversary date Company contributions and earnings of the Trust will be allocated to the accounts of each participant who has just completed a year of service with such allocations to be as provided in Section VII. Participation continues until service is terminated as provided in Sections XII and XIII. Company contributions and forfeitures will not be allocated to the accounts of a participant who for the plan year has more than 500 hours of service, but less than 1,000 hours of service. Hours of service shall include those hours of service of a participant which are not performed by the participant but which are covered by period of approved absence. Participating service is broken by resignation, discharge or a break-in service. If an employee returns to work on or before the end of an approved absence, his participating service is not broken by the approved absence, and any period of approved absence shall be included within the meaning of service. Failure to return to work on or before the end of an approved absence will terminate service as of the end of the approved absence.

Section V. <u>Company Contributions</u>.

A. For the year ending December 31, 1975, and each subsequent year, Company shall make contributions to the Trust in such amounts as may be determined by its Board of Directors. However, Company contributions for each year shall never be less than the amount required to enable the Trust to discharge its current obligations. The amount of the Company contribution for each year will be established by resolution of the Company's Board of Directors and the resolution will be communicated to the participants on or prior to each anniversary date.

B. Company contributions will be paid in cash, shares of Company stock or other property as the Company's Board of Directors may from time to time determine. Shares of Company stock and other property will be valued at their then fair market value. However, to the extent that the Trust has current obligations, the Company contribution will be paid to the Trust in cash. The Company contribution will be paid to the Trust on or before the date required to make such contribution a deduction on the Company's federal income tax return for the year. No participant shall be required or permitted to make contributions to the Plan or Trust.

Section VI. <u>Investment of Trust Assets</u>.

Company contributions in cash and other cash received by the Trust will be applied to pay any current obligations of the Trust incurred for purchase of Company stock, or may be applied to purchase additional shares of Company stock from current shareholders or shares from the Company. The investment policy of the Plan is designed to invest primarily in Company stock. With due regard to providing for such primary investment policy, the Committee may also direct the Trustee to invest funds under the Plan in insurance policies on the life of any "key man" employee. To the extent funds are available thereafter the Committee may direct the Trustee to invest funds temporarily in savings accounts, certificates of deposit, high-grade short-term securities, stocks, bonds, or investments deemed by the Committee to be desirable for the Trust, or such funds may be held in cash or cash equivalents. All investments will be made by the Trustee only upon the direction of the Committee. All purchases of Company stock shall be made at prices which, in the judgment of the Committee, do not exceed the fair market value of such shares. The determination of fair market value shall be determined in good faith by the Committee in accordance with this Section and in accordance with regulations to be promulgated by the Secretary of Labor pursuant to Section 3(18) of the Act. Company stock may be acquired for cash or on terms. In this regard borrowings are authorized including, but not limited to borrowings to obtain funds to acquire Company stock. Borrowings for other Plan purposes for other than the acquisition of Company stock are also authorized.

Section VII. <u>Allocations to Accounts</u>.

A. The Company stock account of each participant will be credited as of each anniversary date with his allocable share of Company stock (including fractional shares) purchased and paid for by the Trust or contributed in kind by the Company, with forfeitures of Company stock and with stock dividends on Company stock held in his Company stock account.

B. The other investments account of each participant so entitled will be credited (or debited) as of each anniversary date with his share of the net income (or loss) of the Trust, with cash dividends on Company stock in his Company stock account and with Company contributions and forfeitures in other than Company stock. It will be debited for any payments on purchases of Company stock or for repayment of debt (including principal and interest) incurred for the purchase of Company stock and with his share of insurance premium payments, if any.

C. The allocations will be made as follows:

1. <u>Employer Contributions</u> - Company contributions will be allocated as of each anniversary date among the accounts of participants so entitled in the ratio in which the covered compensation of each bears to the aggregate covered compensation of all such participants for that year.

2. <u>Forfeitures</u> - Forfeitures will be allocated as of each anniversary date among the accounts of remaining participants so entitled in the ratio in which the covered compensation of each bears to the aggregate covered compensation of all such participants for that year.

3. <u>Net Income (or Loss) of the Trust</u> - The net income (or loss) of the Trust will be determined annually as of each anniversary date. A share thereof will be allocated to each participant's other investments account in the ratio in which the balance of his other investments account on the preceding anniversary date bears to the sum of the balances for the other investment accounts of all participants on that date. The net income (or loss) includes the increase (or decrease) in the fair market value of assets of the Trust (other than Company stock in the Company stock accounts), interest, dividends, other income and expenses attributable to assets in the other investments accounts since the preceding anniversary date. It does not include the interest paid under any installment contract for the purchase of Company stock by the Trust or on any loan used by the Trust to purchase Company stock.

4. *Life Insurance Policies* - In the event that the Committee directs the Trustee to invest in a life insurance policy on the life of any "key man" employee, such policy shall be held as an investment for the benefit of the Trust. Premium payments on any such policy shall be debited to the other investments accounts of participants, as of the anniversary date immediately following payment thereof, in the same ratio as Company contributions for that year are credited to the Company stock accounts of participants. Death proceeds received on any life insurance policy (or Company stock purchased with such proceeds) shall be allocated among the accounts of participants in the ratio in which the total premium payments (for that policy) debited to the other investments account of each current participant bears to the total of such debits for all participants as of the next anniversary date.

5. *Equitable Allocations* - The Committee shall establish accounting procedures for the purpose of making the allocations, valuations and adjustments to participants accounts provided for in this Section. Should the Committee determine that the strict application of its accounting procedures will not result in an equitable and non-discriminatory allocation among the accounts of participants, it may modify its procedures for the purpose of achieving an equitable and non-discriminatory allocation in accordance with the general concepts of the Plan and the provisions of this Section, provided however that such adjustments to achieve equity shall not reduce the vested portion of a participant's interest.

D. The Committee shall establish and maintain separate individual accounts for each participant in the Plan. Separate accounts shall be maintained for all inactive participants who have an interest in the Plan. Such separate accounts shall not require a segregation of the Trust assets and no participant shall acquire any right to or interest in any specific asset of the Trust as a result of the allocations provided for in the Plan. All allocations will be made as of the anniversary date referred to in this Section.

E. *Limitations On Annual Additions*

1. Subject to the adjustments hereinafter set forth, the maximum annual addition to a participant's account shall in no event exceed the lesser of:

>   (a) $25,000 or
>
>   (b) 25% of the participant's annual compensation.

   2. For the purposes of paragraph 1. above the term "annual addition" shall mean the sum for any year of the following amounts:

>   (a) Company contributions; and
>
>   (b) Forfeitures arising from termination of employment of a participant.

   3. The limitation of $25,000 imposed by paragraph 1.(a) above shall be adjusted annually for increases in the cost of living in accordance with Regulations issued by the Secretary of the Treasury pursuant to the provisions of Section 415(d) of the Code.

Section VIII. <u>Expenses of the Plan and Trust.</u>

   The Company shall pay all costs of administering the Plan and any similar expenses of the Trustee not including interest and normal brokerage charges which are included in the costs of securities purchased (or charged to proceeds in the case of sales).

Section IX. <u>Voting Company Stock.</u>

   All Company stock in a Company stock account shall be voted by the Trustee in accordance with instructions from the respective participants. All other Company stock held by the Trustee shall be voted by the Trustee in accordance with instructions from the Committee. The Committee shall not exercise its power to vote any stock for which it has not received instructions.

Section X. <u>Annual Statement.</u>

   As soon as possible after each anniversary date, but in any event no later than 210 days thereafter, each participant will receive a written statement showing as of the anniversary date and in comparative form for the prior year:

A. The balance in each of his accounts as of the preceding anniversary date.

B. The amount of Company contributions and forfeitures allocated to his accounts for the year.

C. The adjustment to his accounts to reflect his share of dividends and the income and expenses of the Trust for the year.

D. The new balances in each of his accounts, including the number of shares of Company stock.

E. Such other information as may be required under the Act, the Code and regulations thereunder.

F. The annual statement may be delivered to the participants in two parts, the first part containing the material in items A, B, C and D above and the second part containing material in item E above plus, if required by the Act or the regulations thereunder, another copy of items A, B, C and D.

WHAT PARTICIPANTS WILL RECEIVE

Section XI. <u>Plan Benefit.</u>

When participation in the Plan terminates, a participant has vested interest in all, a part, or none of the final balances in his Company stock account and in his other investments account in accordance with the provisions of Sections XII and XIII. A participant's vested interest in such accounts under the Plan is called his plan benefit.

Section XII. <u>Plan Benefit at Retirement or Death.</u>

Participation terminates as of the anniversary date coinciding with or next following a participant's retirement or death. In such event a participant's plan benefit will be the total of his account balances as of that anniversary date.

A participant will be treated as having retired under the Plan if his service ends through any of the following:

NORMAL RETIREMENT - A participant's normal retirement date is his 65th birthday.

DEFERRED RETIREMENT - A participant may continue in the service of Company beyond his normal retirement date only upon request of the Company or at his request with Company approval. During any such periods, he shall continue to participate in the Plan until actual retirement.

EARLY RETIREMENT - With the approval of Company, a participant may retire prior to his 65th birthday provided he has completed five years of service.

DISABILITY RETIREMENT - If the Committee determines in a uniform, non-discriminatory manner on the basis of a doctor's certificate that a participant has become permanently disabled to work as a full-time employee, he will be given a disability retirement without regard to his age or length of service.

Section XIII. Other Termination of Service.

    A. If a participant's service terminates for any reason other than death or retirement (as provided in Section XII), his participation in the Plan will terminate as of the anniversary date coinciding with or immediately preceding the date his service terminates if during the plan year in which termination occurs the participant has less than 1,000 hours of service; if during the plan year in which termination occurs the participant has 1,000 or more hours of service his participation will terminate as of the anniversary date coinciding with or next following the termination. If his service terminates because of a one year break-in-service, then his participation will terminate as of the first day of the year in which the break-in-service occurs. His plan benefit will be determined on the basis of the length of his vested service in the Plan in accordance with the following vesting schedule:

Vested Service At Date of Termination	Percent of Accounts Vested
Less than Three Years	0%
Three Years	15%
Four Years	20%
Five Years	25%
Six Years	30%
Seven Years	35%
Eight Years	40%
Nine Years	45%
Ten Years	50%
Eleven Years	60%
Twelve Years	70%
Thirteen Years	80%
Fourteen Years	90%
Fifteen Years	100%

B. If a participant has had a break-in-service of one year or more, then any participating service after such break-in-service will not increase participant's vesting percentage in pre-break accrued benefits.

C. Any part of the final balances in a participant's accounts which does not become part of his plan benefit is a forfeiture. All forfeitures are reallocated among the remaining participants who are entitled to share in contributions for that year. (See Section VII.)

Section XIV. When Plan Benefit Will Be Distributed.

A. A participant's plan benefit will be computed as soon as possible after the anniversary date on which his participation ends. His plan benefit will normally be distributed within one year after his participation ends. Distribution may be made in one of the following alternative modes of distribution, as determined in the sole discretion of the Committee, exercised in a uniform and non-discriminatory manner:

    1. With the participant's consent distribution of his plan benefit in a single distribution, or

      2. Distribution of his plan benefit in substantially equal annual, quarterly or monthly installments plus accrued net income (or loss). This may be based on a fixed number of years or a fixed percentage of his plan benefit. However, the period of installments may not exceed his life expectancy, or the joint life expectancy of him and his spouse, or

      3. Any combination of the foregoing to which the participant consents.

      4. The Committee shall have the right to direct that distribution to participants who terminate service for any reason other than retirement or death shall be deferred and distributed no later than their normal retirement date.

B.   In any event, as provided in Code section 401(b)(14):

      "Unless the participant otherwise elects, the payment of benefits to the participant will begin not later than the 60th day after the latest of the close of the plan year in which —

      "(a) the date on which the participant attains the earlier of age 65 or the normal retirement age specified under the plan

      "(b) occurs the 10th anniversary of the year in which the participant commenced participation in the plan, or

      "(c) the participant terminates his service with the employer."

C.   Any part of a participant's plan benefit which is retained in the Trust after the anniversary date on which his participation ends will continue to be treated as a Company stock account or as an other investments account, as the case may be, as provided in Section VII. However, neither account will be credited with any further Company contributions or forfeitures, nor shall his accounts share in the allocations provided for in Section VII C.4.

Section XV. <u>How Plan Benefit Will be Distributed.</u>

    A. Distribution of plan benefit will be made entirely in whole shares of Company stock. Any balance in a participant's other investments account will be applied to acquire for distribution the maximum number of whole shares of Company stock at the then fair market value. Any fractional share value unexpended balance will be distributed in cash. If Company stock is not available for purchase by the Trustee then the Trustee shall hold such balance until Company stock is acquired and then make such distribution. The Trustee will make distribution from the Trust only on instructions from the Committee.

    B. Distribution will be made to the participant if living, and if not, to his beneficiary. A participant may designate his beneficiary upon becoming a participant, and may change such designation at any time, by filing a written designation with the Committee. Upon the death of a participant, if there is no designated beneficiary then living, or if the designation is not effective for any reason, as determined by the Committee, the participant's beneficiary shall be his surviving spouse, or if none, his surviving children, or if none, such other heirs, or the executor or administrator of his estate, as the Committee shall select.

    C. If the Committee determines that a person entitled to any distribution is physically unable or mentally incompetent to receive such distribution, it may direct the Trustee to apply such distribution for such person's benefit.

    D. The right of any participant or his beneficiary in any benefit as to any payment hereunder or to any separate account shall not be subject to alienation, assignment or transfer voluntarily or involuntarily by operation of law or otherwise except as may be expressly permitted herein and no participant shall assign, transfer, or dispose of such right nor shall any such right be subjected to attachment, execution, garnishment, sequestration, or other legal, equitable, or other process.

Section XVI. <u>Restrictions on Distributed Shares of Company Stock.</u>

    Shares of Company stock distributed by the Trustee may be restricted as to sale or transfer of such shares by the By-Laws or Articles of Incorporation of Company, which restrictions will be similarly applicable to all shares of stock of Company of the same class.

Section XVII. <u>Advance Distributions and Dividends.</u>

    A. Except as otherwise provided in this Section XVII, a participant is not entitled to any payment, withdrawal or distribution under the Plan during his participation.

B. Cash dividends on shares of Company stock allocated to participants' accounts may be paid to participants currently, or from time to time in periodic payments, as determined in the sole discretion of the Committee, exercised in a uniform and non-discriminatory manner.

C. To mitigate any financial hardship to a participant or his beneficiary after his service has ended and before his plan benefit is distributable, the Committee acting in a non-discriminatory manner may direct the Trustee to advance to him or to his beneficiary a partial distribution in Company stock of his plan benefit. If any such partial distribution is made, the participant's plan benefit when computed will be reduced by the amount of any such advance.

GENERAL PROVISIONS

Section XVIII. Administration.

A. The Plan will be administered by a Committee composed of three (3) individuals appointed by the Board of Directors of the Company to serve at its pleasure and without compensation. The Board of Directors shall have no responsibility for the operation and administration of the Plan. The Committee is the named Fiduciary and Administrator of the Plan as provided by the Act and shall have authority to manage and control the operation of the Plan. The Committee may employ investment managers and advisors, accountants, legal counsel, consultants and any other person or organization it feels necessary or proper to assist it in the performance of its duties under the Plan. All reasonable expenses thereof shall be paid as provided in Section VIII. Each member of the Committee and any other person to whom any fiduciary responsibility with respect to the Plan is allocated or delegated shall discharge his duties and responsibilities with respect to the Plan in accordance with the standards set forth in section 404(a)(1) of the Act which provides:

> "Subject to sections 403(c) and (d), 4042 and 4044, a fiduciary shall discharge his duties with respect to a plan solely in the interest of the participants and beneficiaries -
>
> "(a) for the exclusive purpose of:
>
> "(i) providing benefits to participants and their beneficiaries; and

"(ii) defraying reasonable expenses of administering the plan;

"(b) with the care, skill, prudence, and diligence under the circumstances then prevailing that a prudent man acting in a like capacity and familiar with such matters would use in the conduct of an enterprise of a like character and with like aims;

"(c) by diversifying the investments of the plan so as to minimize the risk of large losses, unless under the circumstances it is clearly prudent not to do so; and

"(d) in accordance with the documents and instruments governing the plan insofar as such documents and instruments are consistent with the provisions of this title."

Except however, that the diversification requirement of paragraph (c) and the prudence requirement (only to the extent that it requires diversification) of paragraph (1) will not be violated by the acquisition or holding of Company stock.

B. Committee action shall be by vote of two (2) or more members at a meeting or in writing without a meeting. Minutes of each meeting shall be kept. The Committee may establish such rules as may be necessary or desirable for its own operations. Any Committee member having any interest in a transaction being voted upon by the Committee shall not vote thereon nor participate in the decision.

C. The Committee shall administer the Plan in a uniform, non-discriminatory manner for the exclusive benefit of the participants and their beneficiaries. The Committee shall establish and maintain accounts and records to record the interest of each participant, inactive participant and their respective beneficiaries in the Plan. The Committee shall make such rules, regulations, interpretations, discussions and computations as may be necessary. Its decision on all individual matters will be final. However, any participant whose interest is directly affected by a Committee interpretation or decision shall be notified in writing and the same provisions therefore shall apply as set forth hereinafter in paragraph G.

D. The Committee shall have all powers which are reasonably necessary to carry out its responsibilities under the Plan. It may act as provided herein and shall give instructions to the Trustee on all matters within its discretion as provided in the Trust agreement.

...ions and directions of the Committee may be
... Trustee, to a participant, to the Company or
... who is to receive such decision or direction
... by one member of the Committee and such
... ...ction may be relied upon by its recipient as
being the binding decision or direction of the Committee.

      F.   The Company shall obtain, pay for and keep current a policy or policies of insurance insuring the Plan, the members of the Board of Directors, the Committee and any other person to whom any fiduciary responsibility with respect to the Plan is allocated or delegated from and against any and all liabilities, costs and expenses incurred by such persons as a result of any act or omission to act in connection with the performance of their duties, responsibilities and obligations under the Plan and under the Act.

      G.   All applications for benefits under the Plan shall be submitted to the personnel department of the Company. Applications for benefits must be in writing on the forms prescribed by the Committee and must be signed by the Participant and if required by the Committee his spouse, or in the case of a death benefit, by the beneficiary or legal representative of the deceased Participant. The Committee reserves the right to require that the Participant furnish proof of his age prior to processing any application. Each application shall be acted upon and approved or disapproved within sixty (60) days following its receipt by the personnel department. In the event any application for benefits is denied, in whole or in part, the Company shall notify the applicant in writing of such denial and of his right to a review by the Committee and shall set forth in a manner calculated to be understood by the applicant, specific reasons for such denial, specific references to pertinent Plan provisions on which the denial is based, a description of any additional material or information necessary for the applicant to perfect his application, an explanation of why such material or information is necessary and an explanation of the Plan's review procedure and the method of appeal from the decision.

Section XIX.   *Guarantees.*

      All Plan benefits will be paid only from the Trust assets and neither the Company, the Committee nor the Trustee shall have any duty or liability to furnish the Trust with any funds, securities or other assets except as expressly provided in the Plan. Nothing herein shall be construed to obligate the Company to continue to employ any employee.

Section XX. *Future of the Plan*.

    A. In the event that this Plan and t[...]
or consolidates with, or transfers its assets o[...]
any other qualified plan of deferred compensati[...]
pant shall (if the Plan then terminates) receiv[...]
diately after the merger, consolidation or tran[...]
to or greater than the benefit he would have be[...]
ceive immediately before the merger, consolidat[...]
if this Plan had then been terminated.

    B. The Board of Directors reserves the right to amend the Plan at any time but no amendment shall (a) reduce the benefits of any Participant accrued under the Plan to the date the amendment is adopted, except to the extent that a reduction in accrued benefits may be permitted by the Act or (b) divert any part of the assets of the Trust Fund to purposes other than for the exclusive benefit of the Participants, retired Participants or their beneficiaries who have an interest in the Plan or for the purpose of defraying the reasonable expenses of administering the Plan.

    C. The Company further reserves the right to terminate the Plan and the Trust in the event of failure of the Internal Revenue Service, after application, initially to determine that the Plan and the Trust meet the requirements of section 401(a) of the Code. In that event, all Company contributions together with any income received or accrued thereon less any benefits or expenses paid shall, upon written direction of the Committee be returned to Company notwithstanding the provisions of the Trust, and this Plan shall then terminate.

    D. As future conditions cannot be foreseen, the Company reserves the right to terminate this Plan at any time. Termination shall not retroactively reduce the rights of Participants nor permit any part of the Trust assets to be diverted or used for any purpose other than for the exclusive benefit of the Participants and their beneficiaries. If the Plan is terminated (other than by merger, consolidation or transfer to another qualified Plan as hereinbefore set forth in paragraph A.) by the Company, participation of its employees will end on the anniversary date coinciding with or next following such termination. In the event of such termination, if the Plan is not replaced by a comparable plan qualified under section 401(a) of the Code, the accounts of all Participants affected by the termination will become nonforfeitable as of that anniversary date. A complete and permanent discontinuance of Company contributions shall be deemed a termination of the Plan for this purpose.

After termination of the Plan, the Committee and the Trust will continue until the Plan benefit of each participant has been distributed. Plan benefits may be distributed promptly after they are computed or distribution may be deferred as provided in Section XIV, as the Committee may direct.

Section XXI. Governing Law.

The provisions of this Plan shall be construed, administered and enforced in accordance with the laws of the Act and, to the extent applicable, the State of California. All contributions to the Trust shall be deemed to take place in the State of California.

Section XXII. Execution.

To record the adoption of this Plan, the Company has caused its appropriate officers to affix its corporate name and seal hereto this 25th day of January, 1975.

JONES MANUFACTURING, INC.

By_____
          President

By_____
          Secretary

39.

Sample Of An Employee Stock Ownership Trust Agreement

The Trust Agreement that follows is not a "Model" Trust. It is designed to meet most, but not necessarily all of the requirements arising under ERISA. Certain incorporations by reference of ERISA provisions may have to be set forth in full. Therefore, this Trust must be examined in relation to ERISA and to the regulations under ERISA when they are issued. Such regulations will probably require drastic changes in many provisions set forth and the addition or deletion of other provisions. This Trust should be treated with caution by counsel as being merely a series of suggestions to them and should not be used except by attorneys who can modify this Trust to meet all ERISA requirements to fit the needs of their clients and who become reasonably competent in the specific requirements of ERISA and Trusts which are part of qualified plans.

Marvin Goodson, Esq.
Marvin Goodson Professional Corp.
Los Angeles, California

JONES MANUFACTURING, INC.

EMPLOYEE STOCK OWNERSHIP TRUST AGREEMENT

THIS AGREEMENT, between JONES MANUFACTURING, INC., a California corporation (herein "Company") and _____ _____BANK AND TRUST COMPANY, a California banking corporation (herein "Trustee"), to be effective as of January 1, 1975;

W I T N E S S E T H:

WHEREAS, it is the policy of the Company to so finance and conduct its operations as to enable its employees to acquire through a stock bonus plan equity ownership in the Company; and

WHEREAS, the Company has adopted the "Jones Manufacturing, Inc. Employee Stock Ownership Plan," (herein "Plan") effective as of January 1, 1975; and

WHEREAS, the Company has designated the Plan and this Trust as constituting part of a plan intended to qualify under section 401(a) of the Internal Revenue Code;

NOW, THEREFORE, the parties hereto do hereby establish the Jones Manufacturing, Inc. Employee Stock Ownership Trust as the Trust under the Jones Manufacturing, Inc. Employee Stock Ownership Plan and agree that the following shall constitute the Trust Agreement:

A. **The Trust Assets.**

(1) Employer contributions shall be paid to the Trustee from time to time in accordance with the Plan. All employer contributions hereafter made and all investments thereof, together with all accumulations, accruals, earnings and income with respect thereto shall be held by the Trustee in trust hereunder as the trust assets. The trust assets shall be received by the Trustee and invested pursuant to written instructions to the Trustee from the Committee. The Trustee shall not be responsible for the administration of the Plan, maintaining any records of participants' accounts under the Plan, or the computation of or collection of employer contributions, but shall hold, invest, reinvest, manage, administer and distribute the trust assets as provided herein for the exclusive benefit of participants, retired participants and their beneficiaries.

(2) Unless otherwise directed by the Company or the Committee provided for in the Plan (herein "Committee"), the Trustee shall hold, invest and administer the trust assets as a single fund without identification of any part of the trust assets with or allocation of any part of the trust assets to the Company or to any participant or group of participants of the Company or their beneficiaries.

B. <u>Investment</u>.

(1) As directed by the Committee, the Trustee shall invest and reinvest the trust assets without distinction between principal and income in Company stock in accordance with the terms of the Plan and this Agreement. The Trustee shall also, as directed by the Committee, invest in insurance policies on the life of any "key-man" employee, place funds in savings accounts or in Certificates of Deposit issued by any bank (including Trustee) or savings and loan association, invest in stocks, shares and obligations of corporations or of unincorporated associations or trusts or investment companies or in any kind of investment fund, (including Trustee's pooled investment funds) mutual fund (open-end or otherwise) or common trust fund, or in realty or personalty, including purchase and leaseback transactions, interests in oil or other depletable natural resources and any other kind of investments which are legal and prudent investments for trustees.

(2) The Committee shall assume responsibility and be liable for the making of prudent investments to the extent prescribed in this paragraph and as is more particularly set forth in the Plan. Investments directed by the Committee shall not be in conflict with the "Prohibited Transactions" provisions of the Internal Revenue Code (herein "Code") as currently defined and as hereafter amended or with the provisions of the Employee Retirement Income Security Act of 1974 as currently defined and as hereafter amended (herein "Act"). As directed by the Committee, the Trustee shall purchase such securities or other property, including shares of stock of any classification issued by the Company or shall sell such securities or other property held as part of the trust assets, as may be specified in any such direction. The Trustee shall have no obligation whatsoever to seek or request any such direction from the Committee, nor shall the Trustee have any power or authority to dispose of any securities or property acquired pursuant to such direction unless directed by the Committee. The Trustee shall, subject to the limitations hereinafter set forth, be under a duty to comply with any such direction when given, but shall have no responsibility whatsoever in connection with any such purchase, retention, sale or other act set forth in such direction other than compliance with such direction; provided however:

(a) The Trustee shall not participate knowingly in or knowingly undertake to conceal an act or omission of any other fiduciary to the Plan (as fiduciary is defined in section 3(21) of the Act) knowing such act or omission is a breach;

(b) The Trustee shall not conduct itself in the administration of its specific responsibilities hereunder which give rise to its status as a fiduciary so as to enable another fiduciary to commit a breach;

(c) If the Trustee has knowledge of a breach by any other fiduciary to the Plan, the Trustee shall make reasonable efforts under the circumstances to remedy the breach;

(d) The Trustee shall not follow the directions of the Committee if the Trustee knows, or from the facts of which it is aware should know that the directions are not made in accordance with the terms of the Plan or are contrary to provisions of the Act or the Code;

(3) In the event the Trustee invests any part of the fund, pursuant to the directions of the Committee, in any shares of stock issued by the Company and the Committee thereafter directs the Trustee to dispose of such investment, or any part thereof, under circumstances which, in the opinion of counsel for the Trustee, require registration of the securities under the Securities Act of 1933 and/or qualification of the securities under the Blue Sky laws of any state or states, then the Company at its own expense, will take or cause to be taken any and all such action as may be necessary or appropriate to effect such registration and/or qualification.

C. <u>Trustee's Powers</u>. As directed by the Committee, the Trustee shall have the authority and power to:

(1) sell, transfer, mortgage, pledge, lease or otherwise dispose of, or grant options with respect to any securities or other property in the Trust at public or private sale, for cash or on credit, upon such conditions, at such prices and in such manner as the Committee shall direct, and no person dealing with the Trustee shall be bound to see to the application of the purchase money or to inquire into the validity, expediency or propriety of any such sale or other disposition;

(2) borrow from any lender to acquire Company stock or any other property authorized by this Agreement, giving its note as Trustee with such interest and security for the loan as may be appropriate and necessary and not be prohibited under the Act or the Code;

(3) vote upon any stocks, including Company stock as prescribed in Paragraph D of this Agreement, bonds or other securities held in the Trust, or otherwise consent to or request any action on the part of the issuer in person or by proxy;

(4) give general or specific proxies or powers of attorney with or without powers of substitution;

(5) consent to or otherwise participate in reorganizations, recapitalizations, consolidations, mergers and similar transactions with respect to Company stock or any other securities and to pay any assessments or charges in connection therewith;

(6) deposit such Company stock or other securities in any voting trust, or with any protective or like committee, or with a trustee or with depositories designated thereby;

(7) sell or exercise any options, subscription rights and conversion privileges and to make any payments incidental thereto;

(8) sue, defend, compromise, arbitrate or settle any suit or legal proceeding or any claim, debt or obligation due to or from it as Trustee and to reduce the rate of interest on, extend or otherwise modify, or to foreclose upon default or otherwise enforce any such obligation; to bid in property on foreclosure or to take a deed in lieu of foreclosure with or without paying consideration therefor and in connection therewith to release the obligation on the bond secured by the mortgage;

(9) retain, acquire or otherwise deal in any stock for which it is registrar or transfer agent.

(10) Contract or otherwise enter into transactions between itself as Trustee and as a bank, between itself as Trustee and the Company, or between itself as Trustee and any other institution for which it then, therefore or thereafter may be acting as Trustee;

(11) perform all acts which the Trustee shall deem necessary and appropriate and exercise any and all powers and authority of the Trustee under this Agreement;

(12) exercise any of the powers of an owner, with respect to such Company stock and other securities or other property comprising the trust assets. The Committee, with the Trustee's approval, may authorize the Trustee to act on any administrative matter or class of matters with respect to which direction or instruction to the Trustee by the Committee is called for hereunder without specific direction or other instruction from the Committee.

D. <u>Voting Company Stock</u>. The Trustee shall vote all Company stock held by it as part of the trust assets at such time and in such manner as the Committee shall direct, which direction shall be in accordance with the terms of the Plan which provide for directions to be received by the Committee from participants as to some stock in the Trust; provided, however, that if any agreement entered into by the Trust provides for voting of any shares of Company stock pledged as security for any obligation of the Trust, then such shares of Company stock shall be voted in accordance with such agreement. If the Committee shall fail or refuse to give the Trustee timely instructions as to how to vote any Company stock as to which the Trustee otherwise has the right to vote, the Trustee shall not exercise its power to vote such Company stock.

E. <u>Nominees</u>. The Trustee may register any securities or other property held by it hereunder in its own name or in the name of it's nominees with or without the addition of words indicating that such securities are held in a fiduciary capacity, and may hold any securities in bearer form, but the books and records of the Trustee shall at all times show that all such investments are part of the Trust.

F. <u>Records</u>. The Trustee shall keep accurate and detailed accounts of all investments, receipts and disbursements and other transactions hereunder, and all accounts, books and records relating thereto shall be open to inspection by any person designated by the Committee or the Company at all reasonable times. The Trustee shall maintain such records, make such computations except as concerns employer and employee contributions and perform such ministerial acts as the Committee may from time to time request.

G. <u>Reports</u>.

(1) Within ninety (90) days after the end of each January 31st or the removal or resignation of the Trustee, and as of any other date specified by the Committee, the Trustee shall file a report with the Committee. This report shall show all purchases, sales, receipts, disbursements, and other transactions effected by the Trustee during the year or period for which the report is filed, and shall contain an exact description, the cost as shown on the

Trustee's books, and where readily ascertainable, the market value as of the end of such period, of every item held in the Trust and the amount and nature of every obligation owed by the Trust. For purposes of determining the market value of securities held by the Trustee, such securities shall be valued as of the close of business on such anniversary date or other date or, if securities shall not have been traded and reported on an established securities exchange or in the over-the-counter market on such date, then as of the close of business on the day first preceding such date on which securities shall have been traded and reported.

(2) Notwithstanding any other provision of this paragraph G, if the Trustee shall determine that the trust assets consist in whole or in part of property not traded freely on a recognized market, including but not limited to Company stock or that information necessary to ascertain the fair market value thereof is not readily available to the Trustee, the Trustee shall request the Committee to instruct the Trustee as to the value of such property for all purposes under the Plan and this Agreement, and the Committee shall comply with such request. The value placed upon such property by the Committee in its instructions to the Trustee shall be conclusive and binding upon the Trustee subject to the provisions of paragraph B(2) herein. If the Committee shall fail or refuse to instruct the Trustee as to the value of such property within a reasonable time after receipt of the Trustee's request to do so, the Trustee may engage a competent appraiser to fix the fair market value of such property for all purposes hereunder. The determination of any such appraiser as to the fair market value of such property shall be the value reported hereunder and the Trustee shall have no liability in connection therewith subject to the provisions of paragraph B(2) herein. The reasonable fees and expenses incurred for any such appraisal shall be deemed an expense of the Trustee and paid as provided in the Plan.

H. <u>Distributions</u>.

(1) The Trustee shall make distributions from the Trust at such times and in such number of shares of Company stock and amounts of cash to or for the benefit of the person entitled thereto under the Plan as the Committee directs in writing. Any undistributed part of a participant's interest in his accounts shall be retained in the Trust until the Committee directs its distribution. Where distribution is directed in Company stock, the Trustee shall cause an appropriate certificate to be issued to the person entitled thereto and mailed to the address furnished it by the Committee. Any portion of a participant's account to be dis-

tributed in cash shall be paid by the Trustee mailing its check to the same person at the same address. If a dispute arises as to who is entitled to or should receive any benefit or payment, the Trustee may withhold or cause to be withheld such payment until the dispute has been resolved.

(2) As directed by the Committee, the Trustee shall make payments out of the trust assets. Such directions or instructions need not specify the purpose of the payments so directed and the Trustee shall not be responsible in any way respecting the purpose or propriety of such payments except for the provisions of paragraph B(2).

(3) No distribution or payment under this Agreement to any participant or his beneficiary under the Plan shall be subject in any manner to anticipation, sale, transfer, assignment or encumbrance, whether voluntary or involuntary, and no attempt so to anticipate, sell, transfer, assign or encumber the same shall be valid or recognized by the Trustee, nor shall any such distribution or payment be in any way liable for or subject to the debts, contracts, liabilities or torts of any person entitled to such distribution or payment, except to such extent as may be required by law or expressly provided for in the Plan. If the Trustee is notified by the Committee that any such participant or beneficiary has been adjudicated bankrupt or has purported to anticipate, sell, transfer, assign or encumber any such distribution or payment, voluntarily or involuntarily, the Trustee shall, if so directed by the Committee, hold or apply such distribution or payment or any part thereof to or for the benefit of such participant or beneficiary in such manner as the Committee shall direct.

(4) In the event that any distribution or payment directed by the Committee shall be mailed by the Trustee to the person specified in such direction at the latest address of such person filed with the Committee, and shall be returned to the Trustee because such person cannot be located at such address, the Trustee shall promptly notify the Committee of such return. Upon the expiration of sixty (60) days after such notification, such direction shall become void and unless and until a further direction by the Committee is received by the Trustees with respect to such distribution or payment, the Trustee shall thereafter continue to administer the Trust as if such direction had not been made by the Committee. The Trustee shall not be obligated to search for or ascertain the whereabouts of any such person.

I. *Signatures.* All communications required hereunder from the Company or the Committee to the Trustee shall be in writing signed by an officer of the Company or a person authorized by the Committee to sign on its behalf. The Committee shall authorize one or more individuals to sign on its behalf all communications required hereunder between the Committee and the Trustee. The Company and the Committee shall at all times keep the Trustee advised of the names and specimen signatures of all members of the Committee and the individuals authorized to sign on behalf of the Committee. The Trustee shall be fully protected in relying on any such communication and shall not be required to verify the accuracy or validity thereof unless it has reasonable grounds to doubt the authenticity of any signature. If after request the Trustee does not receive instructions from the Committee on any matter in which instructions are required hereunder, subject to the provisions of paragraph D hereof, the Trustee shall act or refrain from acting as it may determine. All communications required hereunder from the Trustee shall be in writing signed by the Trustee.

J. *Expenses.* The Trustee and the Committee may employ suitable agents and counsel who may be counsel for the Company. The expenses incurred by the Trustee and the Committee in the performance of their duties hereunder and all other proper charges, expenses and disbursements of the Trustee or the Committee, including the Trustee's compensation, shall be paid by the Company, provided that if the Company is unable to pay the same, or fails to do so, they may be charged to and paid out of the trust assets. However, normal brokerage charges, commissions, taxes and other costs incident to the purchase and sale of securities which are included in the cost of securities purchased, or charged against the proceeds in the case of sales, shall be charged to and paid out of trust assets. The Trustee shall be entitled to compensation as may be agreed upon in writing from time to time between the Committee and Trustee.

K. *Liability of Trustee.* The Trustee shall not be liable for any expense or liability hereunder unless due to or arising from fraud, dishonesty, negligence, misconduct of the Trustee or arising from acts which are in violation of the Trustee's duties as set forth in paragraph B(2) herein. Except as thus provided, the Trustee shall not be liable for the making, retention or sale of any investment or reinvestment made by the Trustee as herein provided, nor for any loss to or diminution of the trust assets, nor for any action which the Trustee takes or refrains from taking at the direction of the Committee. Except as thus provided the Trustee shall not be liable for the making, retention or sale of any investment or reinvestment made by the Trustee as herein provided, nor for any loss to or diminution of the trust assets, nor for any action which the Trustee takes or refrains from taking at the direction of the Committee. Except as thus provided the Trustee shall not be required to pay interest on any part of the trust assets which are held uninvested pursuant to the Committee's direction.

    L.   Amendment and Termination.

(1) The Company shall have the right at any time, by an instrument in writing, duly executed and acknowledged and delivered to the Trustee, to modify, alter or amend this Agreement, in whole or in part, and to terminate the Trust, in accordance with the express provisions of the Plan, provided, however, that the duties, responsibilities and liabilities of the Trustee hereunder shall not be increased without its prior written consent; provided, further, that no amendment hereto shall divert any part of the assets of the Trust Fund to purposes other than for the exclusive benefit of the Participants, retired Participants or beneficiaries or for the purpose of defraying the reasonable expenses of administering the Plan. The Company shall have the right, in said manner, to amend this Agreement retroactively to its effective date in order to initially satisfy the requirements of section 401(a) of the Code and all provisions of the Act, and to terminate this Agreement in the event of failure of the Internal Revenue Service, after application, to determine that the Plan and the Trust initially satisfy the requirements of section 401(a) of the Code. In no event, however, shall the duties, powers or liabilities of the Trustee hereunder be changed without its prior written consent.

(2) It is intended that this Trust and the Plan referred to herein constitute a qualified trust under section 401(a) of the Internal Revenue Code. However, in the event that an initial favorable determination letter from the Internal Revenue Service is not obtained, all contributions together with any income received or accrued thereon less any benefits or expenses paid shall, within one year of the denial, upon written direction of the Company, be returned to the Company, and the Trust shall terminate.

    M.   Irrevocability. Subject to the provisions of paragraph L, this Trust is declared to be irrevocable and at no time shall any part of the trust assets revert to or be recoverable by the Company or be used for or be diverted to purposes other than for the exclusive benefit of Participants or retired or terminated Participants and their beneficiaries. However, the Committee may by notice in writing to the Trustee direct that subject to all prior approvals that may be required of the Internal Revenue Service and the Department of Labor and in accordance with the terms of the Plan as it may from time to time be amended all or part of the trust assets be transferred to a successor Trustee or Trustees under a trust instrument which is for the exclusive benefit of such participants and their beneficiaries and meets the requirements of section 401(a) of the Internal Revenue Code, and thereupon the trust assets or any part thereof, together with any outstanding loans and accrued interest attributable thereto shall be paid over, transferred or assigned to said Trustee or Trustees free from the trust created hereunder; provided, however, that no part of the trust assets may be used to pay premiums or to make contributions of the Company under any other plan maintained by the Company for the benefit of its employees.

N. <u>Resignation or Removal of Trustee.</u>

(1) The Trustee may resign at any time upon thirty (30) days' written notice to the Company. The Trustee may be removed at any time by the Company upon thirty (30) days' written notice to the Trustee. Upon the receipt of instructions or directions from the Company, or the Committee with which a Trustee is unable or unwilling to comply, the Trustee may resign upon notice in writing to the Company or the Committee given within a reasonable time, under the circumstances then prevailing, after the receipt of such instructions or directions, and notwithstanding any other provisions hereof, in that event the Trustee shall have no liability to the Company, or any person interested herein for failure to comply with such instructions or directions. Upon resignation or removal of the Trustee, the Company shall appoint a successor Trustee (or Trustees) which may be a corporate or an individual or individuals. The successor Trustee shall have the same powers and duties as are conferred upon the Trustee hereunder, and the Trustee shall assign transfer and pay over to such successor Trustee all the moneys, securities and other property then constituting the trust assets, together with such records or copies thereof as may be necessary to the successor Trustee.

(2) The Trustee shall not be required to make any transfer under this paragraph N or the preceding paragraph M to a successor Trustee or Trustees unless and until it has been indemnified to its reasonable satisfaction against any expenses and liabilities with respect to such transfer.

O. <u>Definition</u>. The definitions of certain words in the Plan shall apply to this Agreement wherever applicable. Male references include female and the singular or plural number shall each be deemed to include the other whenever the context so indicates.

P. <u>Miscellaneous</u>.

(1) So long as this Plan is in effect, Company shall file with Internal Revenue Service and the Department of Labor, at the time and place required, the information provided for in applicable sections of the Internal Revenue Service Income Tax Regulations and applicable sections of the regulations of the Department of Labor. If this trust and the Plan referred to herein, after initially qualifying as a tax exempt trust under section 401(a) of the Internal Revenue Code shall thereafter cease to be a qualified trust by reason of some act or omission on the part of the Company, the Company agrees to indemnify Trustee and hold Trustee harmless against any liability it may incur for federal estate or other taxes as a result of payments made from the trust to beneficiaries of deceased participants after it ceases to be a qualified trust.

(2) In the event any provisions of this Agreement shall be held illegal or invalid for any reason, the illegality or invalidity shall not affect the remaining provisions of this Agreement, but shall be fully severable and the Agreement shall be construed and enforced as if the illegal or invalid provision had never been inserted herein.

Q. <u>Acceptance</u>. The Trustee hereby accepts this trust and agrees to hold the trust assets existing on the date of this Agreement and all additions and accretions thereto subject to all the terms and conditions of this Agreement which shall be interpreted and construed under the laws of the State of California.

IN WITNESS WHEREOF, the Company and the Trustee have caused this Agreement to be executed in duplicate this_____ day of_____, 1975.

JONES MANUFACTURING, INC.

By_____
      President

By_____
      Secretary

TRUSTEE

_____

40.

Summary

The Employee Stock Ownership Plan is more than just another fringe benefit program. It is also an efficient corporate planning tool and is unusually effective in the implementation of estate planning for stockholders.

> An ESOP is an extraordinary deferred compensation mechanism in that it can provide security for employees in addition to instilling in them a feeling of belonging.

The very act of enriching the employees' future will hopefully enhance the corporation's current and future financial well-being.

Appendix

Tax Code Provisions Relating To ESOT's
(For Use Only By Counsel)

Following are some of the more important tax references that will be encountered in connection with ESOT's. This list is not conclusive, nor are the descriptions of the sections to be considered other than generalities.

All of the regulations pertaining to ESOT's contained in the Employee Retirement Income Security Act of 1974 (ERISA) had not been released by the time this book went to press. Since they may affect portions of this book, they should be reviewed carefully.

IRC Section 401(a)—the general section that covers all tax-qualified plans.

IRC Section 404(a)(3)(A)—limits to 15% the allowable deductible contributions to a stock bonus plan.

Section 408(e) *of the Employee Retirement Income Security Act of 1974 (ERISA)*—permits the ESOT to purchase securities from the corporation and from controlling stockholders, so long as it does so at a fair price.

IRC Sections 404(a)(2) *and* 407(d)(3)(A) *of ERISA*—provisions which are involved in qualifying ESOP's as individual account plans, and make ESOP's exempt from the diversification rule applicable to non-individual account plans.

Section 407(a)—limits the amount of securities and real property of the employer that can be held by pension or profit-sharing plans. ESOT's are exempt from this limitation since they are individual account plans [*IRC Section* 404(a)(2)].

Section 407(d)(3)(B) *of ERISA*—Certain other qualified plans which have not provided for the investment of their funds in employer securities must have been amended prior to January 1, 1976 so that they can invest in employer securities.

Section 2004(a) *of ERISA* [*IRC Section* 415(c)(1)]—covers the limitation on carryovers in the Trust, viz, 25% of a participant's account or $25,000 whichever is less.

Rev. Rul. 71-256, CB 1971-1, 118—distribution of a participant's Plan benefits must be in the form of employer stock.

Section 4021(b)(1) *of ERISA*—relates to plan termination insurance. ESOT's, unlike Fixed Benefit Pension Plans, are exempt from this requirement.

Reg. 1.402(a)-1(b)(1)(ii)—notes that contributions to a stock bonus plan need not depend upon profits.

Reg. 1.401(a)-1(b)(1)(iii)—benefits of a stock bonus plan are to be distributed in stock rather than in cash.

Section 408(b)(3)—permits ESOT's to borrow at a reasonable interest rate with guarantees by employer in order to buy employer stock.

IRC Section 2039(c)(1)—allows benefits of participants to be excluded from Federal Estate Tax.

Reg. 1.1032-1(a)—contributions to a stock bonus Trust can be entirely in employer stock.

IRC Section 1001(b)—contributions to the Trust may be made in non-employer real property or stock as well as in cash or contributions of these.

Appendix

Rev. Rul., 69-65, *I.R.B.* 1969-7, 9—exempts stock bonus plan from the requirement that investments to tax-qualified Trusts provide a fair return.

IRC Section 404(A) through (D)—details fiduciary duties. It is imperative that all sections of ERISA that pertain to the fiduciary responsibility be studied carefully.

IRC Section 318(a)(2)(B), (a)(3)(B)—specifically exclude qualified Trusts from attribution rules.

Section 407(d)(6)(A) *of ERISA*—Definition of ESOP: must be an eligible individual account plan "which is a stock bonus plan which is qualified, or a stock bonus plan and money purchase pension [sic] both of which are qualified ... and which is designed to invest primarily in qualifying employer [sic] securities."

Rev. Rul., 71-311, 1971-2 C.B. 184, *updated Rev. Rul.*, 46-1953-1 C.B. 287-*Sections* 408(b)(3)(A) & (B) *of ERISA*—ESOP's can borrow.

Section 407(e) *of ERISA*—Definition of "marketable obligation."

Section 407(d)(5) *and Section* 407(d)(6)(A) *of ERISA* when read together seem to say that ESOT's can invest primarily in employer marketable obligations.